MOTHERHOOD

MOTHERHOOD

Facing
and
Finding
Yourself

Lisa Marchiano

sounds true
BOULDER, COLORADO

Sounds True
Boulder, CO 80306

Published 2021

Cover design by Jennifer Miles
Book design by Meredith March

The wood used to produce this book is from Forest Stewardship Council (FSC) certified forests, recycled materials, or controlled wood.

Printed in the United States of America

Library of Congress Cataloging-in-Publication Data

Names: Marchiano, Lisa, author.
Title: Motherhood : facing and finding yourself / Lisa Marchiano.
Description: Boulder, CO : Sounds True, 2021. | Includes bibliographical
   references and index.
Identifiers: LCCN 2020054459 (print) | LCCN 2020054460 (ebook)
   | ISBN 9781683646662 (trade paperback) | ISBN 9781683646679 (ebook)
Subjects: LCSH: Motherhood–Psychological aspects. | Mother and child.
   | Self-realization.
Classification: LCC BF723.M55 M37 2021 (print) | LCC BF723.M55
   (ebook) | DDC 155.6/463–dc23
LC record available at https://lccn.loc.gov/2020054459
LC ebook record available at https://lccn.loc.gov/2020054460

10 9 8 7 6 5 4 3 2 1

For my mother.

And my children.

Contents

Preface   ix

Introduction: Journey to the Source   1

PART I: DOWN THE WELL

Chapter 1   Losing Freedom   15

Chapter 2   Losing Control   35

Chapter 3   Losing Ourselves   57

PART II: AT THE BOTTOM

Chapter 4   Encountering Darkness   81

Chapter 5   Valuing Darkness   99

Chapter 6   Embodying Darkness   117

PART III: SURFACING

Chapter 7   Claiming Transcendence   143

Chapter 8   Claiming Creativity   163

Chapter 9   Claiming Authority   183

Epilogue   203

Acknowledgments   207

Appendix   209

Notes   213

Index   221

About the Author   227

Preface

always thought I didn't want children. In college, when a friend confessed a deep longing to become a mother, I couldn't relate. I had ambitious career plans, and being a mother sounded limiting and ordinary. After college, I worked for a nonprofit organization in Washington, DC. My work felt exciting, important, and meaningful. Deep down, I knew there were many things I needed to do in my life, and I feared that having children would prevent me from fulfilling my potential.

Bestselling author and psychologist James Hillman proposed what he called the "acorn theory" of psychological development.[1] He contended that we each enter the world carrying something unique that asks to be lived out through us. Just as the destiny of the oak tree is contained within the acorn, we arrive in life with something we need to do and someone we need to become. "What waits to awaken in each person is ancient and surprising, mythic and meaningful,"[2] writes mythologist and author Michael Meade. As a young woman, I wanted badly to find what was waiting to be awakened. I was afraid that becoming a mother would fatally interrupt its unfolding.

My mother had been frustrated with her role. Though I always felt loved by her, she would at times rail about how limited she had allowed her life to become. "Don't ever have children!" she would shout at us when she felt particularly downtrodden—which was often. I grew up to have ambivalent feelings about motherhood.

Time and age softened my conviction to avoid becoming a mother. Eventually I learned that the conscious part of my personality did not, in fact, have all the answers. At twenty-eight, I was studying international relations in New York. I planned to go to law school next, so that I would be equipped to continue my exciting work with international nonprofits. But some deeper part of myself had other plans. Upon arriving in New York, I began having dream after dream set in the subway. These subterranean dream images mirrored a psychic descent. In spite of my efforts to avoid doing so, I was falling into a depression. The work that had heretofore given my life a sense of purpose and meaning now seemed empty. No matter how I threw myself into graduate school and other aspects of my life, I felt increasingly isolated, sad, and tearful. I was being dragged into the depths against my will.

Though I was terrified of such a descent, by early spring I had been led by my dreams to become curious about what was happening to me. I began writing down my dreams each night and reading books by Jungian authors. These books introduced me to a different way of relating to my unhappiness. They helped me see my suffering and symptoms as an invitation to discover more about myself, and I was gripped by what I was learning.

Carl Jung (1875–1961) was a Swiss psychiatrist and one of the great explorers of the soul. Jung identified several drives but posited that the overarching one was an innate desire to realize one's potential. While he agreed that the unconscious contained elements that were repressed or forgotten, he also felt that the unconscious could be the source of tremendous creativity and growth. He held that we are all connected to a common source of image and meaning through our access to the deep unconscious with its storehouse of universal, archetypal patterns of human experience. In the midst of my depression and confusion, Jung's ideas were a healing balm. My dark and lonely passage became suffused with meaning and purpose.

The depression was a major seismic event that altered the flow of my life energy and shifted its course. I yielded to the urges and instincts that welled up from within. With hindsight, it is clear that my "dark night of the soul" in New York that year was my inborn destiny—my acorn—trying to grow. Within a few years, I set aside my plans to study law and began the long road to becoming a Jungian analyst.

Around this time, I met and married my husband. He had a deep longing to have children, and I had become wise enough to know how to yield to what life offered. Two years after our wedding, I became a mother. To my surprise, the first year of my daughter's life was filled with great fulfillment and joy. After the first few difficult and exhausting months, she and I settled into a wonderful rhythm. I adored everything about caring for her. As if having this beautiful, perfect baby weren't enough, I began my training to become a Jungian analyst just after my daughter turned one. I would push her stroller around the neighborhood, a heavy volume of Jung's *Collected Works* weighing down the diaper bag so that I could sit on a bench and read when she fell asleep. I felt completely whole and content.

But this contentment was short lived. A few months after my daughter turned one, I became pregnant with our second child. The new pregnancy brought with it more exhaustion—and more anxiety. I worried constantly about how the next baby's arrival would affect my life—my work, my analytic training, and my relationship with my daughter.

My son was born a week before my daughter's second birthday. Caring for a toddler and a newborn was draining, and I found myself overwhelmed, exhausted, and depressed. Though I continued to see a small number of patients in my private practice, I was forced to take a leave from my Jungian training program, leaving me feeling adrift, without the sense that I was moving forward in my life professionally. I weighed more than I ever had in my life, and I had no time to exercise or eat thoughtfully. The physical exertion, the third straight year of sleep deprivation, the lack of any time to inhabit my thoughts and inner life, and the sheer impossibility of meeting the demands of an infant and a toddler left me feeling depleted, tearful, and incompetent. With two little kids, I felt as though I were losing myself, getting sucked into the mire.

One cold December day, having gone for a walk just to get out of the house, I struggled to push the kids uphill in the double stroller. *Everything about being a mother is so hard*, I thought to myself. My next thought surprised me: *I'm growing so much as a result. What is happening to me right now must surely be an opportunity to understand myself better.*

It has been over fifteen years since that thought first struck me, and my babies have grown into teenagers. Along the way, it has not ever ceased to be true that parenting is gut-wrenchingly difficult and always offers new insights about myself, if I care to see them. I have learned from my parenting experiences, and I have also been privileged to witness the parenting journeys of mothers in my practice—some of them becoming mothers for the first time, others managing a relationship with their adult child, and everything in between.

Motherhood, with its intense physical and emotional extremes, is a crucible in which we are tested and altered. In the alchemical vessel of motherhood, the heat is turned up high. Outdated parts of our personality are melted away, and new structures are forged. Motherhood is a dizzying high-wire act, a masquerade, and a communion with mortality. It is a falling from and finding of grace, a falling in and out of love, and heartache by the hour. Motherhood is the ultimate confrontation with yourself. Whatever is there to discover at the bottom of your soul, whether dross or treasure, motherhood will help you find it.

One of Jung's most important ideas is that we continue to grow and develop throughout the course of our lives. According to Jung, we never stop growing and changing. In fact, as we age, we have more opportunity to become ourselves—to tend to the unfolding of our unique blueprints, to grow into the oak trees we came into the world with the potential to be. Jung called this lifelong maturation "individuation."

Individuation is the slow process of tuning in to your authentic self. It takes a lifetime. It requires you to stay open to life so that with each blow or disappointment or mistake, you befriend some new part of yourself that had been unknown or despised by you before. If you go through life tending to your authentic voice and making it your job to learn and accept as much about yourself as you can, you generally wind up being one of those older people who are happy and wise, rather than an older person who is bitter and small-minded.

At my first symposium in Jungian training, I had a direct experience of what individuation can look like. The conference, attended by hundreds of analysts and trainees, was in a large hotel in downtown Montreal. It was my first time at such an event, and I felt intimidated at being in close quarters with some of the Jungian authors whose books I had found so influential. Hoping to be a good student, I dutifully attended every lecture despite being exhausted due to being a few months pregnant with baby number two.

Renowned Jungian analyst Harry Wilmer was speaking in the afternoon about yarn paintings. Dr. Wilmer was a pioneer in social psychology who had developed a new technique for working with veterans. Never having before heard of yarn paintings, I assumed Dr. Wilmer would be presenting on artifacts from some indigenous people and discussing the archetypal symbolism found therein. It sounded a little dull, but I was determined to be conscientious.

Wilmer was in his mideighties, and his voice was halting and tentative as he took the microphone. He began by explaining that during World War II, he had been diagnosed with tuberculosis, and had been in a TB sanitarium aboard his naval vessel for nearly a year and a half. This had been a difficult and lonely time for him, and he had felt compelled to take yarn and needle and make "paintings" using a technique that he spontaneously developed. His long illness gave him a deeper understanding of himself, and his yarn paintings reflected this inner process. He showed us several slides of his artwork, revealing his attempts to come to terms with sadness, heartache, and loneliness. He told the story of his adult son dying in a motorcycle accident and showed photographs of yarn paintings completed in the aftermath of this tragedy.

The paintings were colorful and interesting, but their artistic merit was not the point. Wilmer shared how he started sewing from the middle of his "canvas" and never knew how the final result would look. These were spontaneous products of his unconscious, in many ways as simple and artless as a child's. "Everyone at heart is an artist," he said.

At some point early on in the presentation, my tears began to flow, and they never entirely stopped. I had been expecting a dazzling if arcane intellectual discussion from this famous analyst. Instead, a man stood before us entirely undefended and shared his simple efforts to make meaning out of unbearable anguish. I wasn't sure if my tearfulness was in part due to the hormones of early pregnancy. When I ran into a friend later and asked if she had attended, she said simply, "Oh yes. I cried the whole way through."

Harry Wilmer died a year and a half later at the age of eighty-eight.

Jung says that the goal of psychological growth is to become more whole. Becoming whole means being able to experience all of our emotions fully, doubt ourselves, admit our faults, take a passionate interest in the world around us, embrace our ambivalence, hear our inner voice, and marshal our power and authority in the interest of protecting ourselves and those whom we love.

Becoming whole means being able to be playful, feel awe, and laugh at yourself. It means being able to defend yourself when needed but able to drop those defenses at other times so that you are meeting the world around you with an open heart, awake to the wonder and vulnerable to the pain. Maybe most of all, becoming whole involves being curious about yourself so that as you face each new challenge that life presents, you have the opportunity to learn more about the mystery of your soul.

Few other life experiences provide an opportunity to know yourself like being a mother. Being a mother will tire you out, fill you with dread, and move you to tears. It will inspire joy, self-doubt, hilarity, contentment, rage, terror, shame, irritation, inadequacy, grief, anxiety, and love. You will probably see yourself at your very best and your very worst. If, at the end of the day, the point of life is to be made larger by your experiences so that you know more of yourself, motherhood provides a rich arena for self-understanding.

Viewed this way, it doesn't matter whether we are perfect mothers —whether we work or stay home, make our own baby food or sew our own Halloween costumes. What matters is whether we engage in the experience in an openhearted way so that we are *there*, truly present to our own life with all of its heartaches, disappointments, and joys. If you mother in this spirit, you cannot go wrong no matter how many "mistakes" you make. "The right way to wholeness . . ." said Jung, "is full of fateful detours and wrong turnings."[3] If embraced consciously, motherhood can help you become more whole.

If you let it, motherhood will be an opportunity to grow into the fullest version of yourself. But it can be hard to heed this call. We might find ourselves choosing away from the struggle of parenting. Mothering will often bring up difficult feelings that provoke shame, doubt, and sometimes even self-hatred. You may understandably find yourself tempted to avoid these feelings by avoiding your children, either by spending as much time away from them as possible or by emotionally disengaging from them. Or you may silence the promptings of your inner voice and be overly reliant on collective dictums about how to parent. Doing so can relieve the tension of self-doubt, but this relief will come at the sacrifice of authenticity. You will also be missing out on an opportunity to know yourself better. The dark days of motherhood are painful. But it is in these experiences that we stretch our roots right into our deepest ground of being.

Of course, when we are stumbling and sleep-deprived beyond reason as we nurse the baby, it can be hard to remember that we are growing psychologically. When we are heartsick and terrified as our teenager careens into depression or self-harm, an awareness of transformation is hardly the main thing on our mind. It can be difficult to know that our trials have meaning.

Luckily, those who have come before us have left an inexhaustible trove of stories that can serve as guides. We can turn to these to make sense of our experiences, to reassure ourselves that we are not alone, and to connect our travails with their universal expression so that suffering becomes soul-making. Fairy tales are these guiding stories.

A wise person once said that a fairy tale is a story that is false on the outside but true on the inside.[4] Myths and fairy tales are rich storehouses of universal psychic patterns. They illuminate life themes we may struggle with at one time or another. The vast majority of tales have something to say about this process of becoming whole, or individuation, that we have been discussing. When we recognize ourselves in a fairy tale, we know we are not alone. Others have been there before us. Maybe we can see our plight a little differently, or maybe we can imagine more options for ourselves. And we have some sense of where we are going because we know what story we are in. At least, it is a balm to our worried heart to know that whatever struggle we are engaged in is part of the universal human story. We are all, in the end, actors in a divine drama. Hearing our concerns echoed in the beautiful, timeless language of fairy tales and myth is deeply healing.

The hero is one of the two fundamental archetypal patterns that each of us may live out over the course of our lives. The mother is the other one. While the hero is commonly associated with men and the mother with women, both sexes may be called to live out either pattern—or both—over the course of a lifetime. The fundamental aspects of the hero's journey are revealed through the numerous myths and tales in which a hero must venture out into unknown territory, conquer dragons and other challenges, and return with new wisdom. The mother's journey has likewise been elucidated in ancient and timeless tales. Her pattern shares much in common with that of the hero, but it differs in one vital way: hers is not a journey out but a journey down. Heroine stories usually involve a descent.

The symbol of the well frequently occurs in myths and fairy tales. It is a rich image symbolizing contact with the deep, life-giving waters that mysteriously well up from the underworld—the unconscious. In Celtic mythology, sacred wells were points of access to the other world, and their waters had magical or healing properties.

As a child, I spent summers visiting the Georgia farm of my paternal grandparents. Though the house had been fitted with modern plumbing sometime in the 1950s, my grandmother still liked to draw water from the large wooden well that dominated the back porch. A deep well is an uncanny place. I recall the shivery feeling of leaning perilously over the edge. The sense of dizzying depth, the odd echoes, the coolness that wafted up on even the hottest days intimated the existence of another realm. When my grandmother loosed the bucket, the winch unspooled noisily with great rocking vibrations, and the bucket flew down, and down, and down for an impossibly long time before we heard a far distant splash. *The Book of Symbols* tells us that at a well, "we are connected, it seems, to another mysterious realm, underground, underworld, evocative of our own, unknown, reflective depths, a psychic matrix perhaps infinitely extensive."[5]

Year after year, decade upon decade, my grandfather channeled his existential anxieties into a fear that the well would go dry. But the well never did cease to offer up its cold, quenching water. No matter how many times we sent the bucket spinning down into the cool depths, it always came back full. Wells, then, remind us of our connection with the deep, mysterious source of psychic life with its inexhaustible font of intuition, dream, and imagination.

You contain a well that will never run dry, though at times it may not feel like this. The well within connects you to the deep source of wisdom, intuition, and instinct that is the heritage of humankind. The challenges of motherhood are an invitation to connect with this source—to descend into your depths to discover the boundless well-spring of creativity, image, and meaning in the inner world. Though my grandfather always feared the well would go dry if we used too much water, we used to remember that wells were most likely to go dry when they *weren't* used. The gifts of the unconscious are truly limitless—the more you look to the unconscious for wisdom, the more of its abundance you'll receive.

This book will guide you in journeying down this well and drawing from its secret source. Fairy tales, myths, and dreams are aspects of the riches that await you in the following pages as you begin your descent—a descent that will serve as an initiation to your own depths.

Introduction:
Journey to the Source

Consciousness longs for the healing power of nature,
for the deep wells of being and for unconscious
communion with life in all its countless forms.

C. G. JUNG
COLLECTED WORKS, VOL. 5

Any initiatory journey requires a guide, and this book aims to be just that. The stories told in this book map the universal cycle of descent, sojourn, and return that marks a feminine initiation. This cycle will recur for us repeatedly as we come to know ourselves more deeply through mothering. When you first become a mother, when your child starts school, when she faces difficulties as a preteen, or when he leaves for college—all of these experiences may offer an invitation to descend to your source and return changed yet again. In little ways and in big, motherhood will be full of opportunities to know yourself better, and this book endeavors to cover the full range of a mother's psychological journey.

In part one of this book, I will explore how motherhood repeatedly sends us down the well into the marvelous, frightening inner world. The descent is most of all experienced as a loss—a loss of freedom, control, ourselves. In part 2, we will look at the discoveries to be made and the challenges to be faced in this subterranean land. In the sojourn, we will encounter the darkness within, including those despised and repudiated parts of ourselves that are sometimes frightening to know. Finally, in part 3, the return, we will take a closer look at the psychological treasures to which we can hopefully lay claim when we resurface, including mature spirituality, renewed creativity, and an abiding sense of inner authority.

Some of the tales in this book may pierce your heart, speaking to you with great clarity and immediacy. Others may seem strange or difficult to understand. Sometimes those tales that are challenging at first may hold important wisdom that only becomes clear later. As you read, pay attention to the feelings, thoughts, and images that come up for you. You might find it helpful to keep a journal where you can write about your reactions.

You might also pay attention to the dreams that visit you while you read this book. Dreams are the strange language through which your unconscious addresses you. "In each of us there is another whom we do not know," remarked Jung. "He speaks to us in dreams and tells us how differently he sees us from the way we see ourselves."[1] Dreams communicate through metaphor, image, symbol, and feeling. Sometimes frightening, sometimes beautiful, they are always fascinating. Even when we don't understand them, somehow we know that they are meaningful, for they contain the wisdom of the guiding self. They always reveal something we did not consciously know before. Your dreams can be your guide through your motherhood journey. In this book, we will sometimes explore a dream and ponder its significance.

Fairy tales, like dreams, are nourishing if we only enjoy and value them. However, as with dreams, their healing value is made more potent when we engage with them actively. For this reason, I have included questions for reflection at the end of every chapter. To make use of these, first read the tale in full. Then use the questions as prompts for reflection, journaling, or discussion. Just respond with the first answer that comes up for you, even if it doesn't make much sense. The point is to let the imagery of the tale guide you in a conversation with your unconscious. There are no wrong answers.

Mothering is one of life's great opportunities to submit to the fires of transformation. Such a transformation brings with it enormous psychological wealth as we grow into the person we were meant to become. But there can be no doubt that transformation is often painful, lonely, and frightening. Most of us will face dark moments at least occasionally as we mother, though it can feel forbidden to speak of them. Darkness will always be part of a descent, and this is why many of the tales in this book have dark themes. As you follow the promptings of your soul and go down into the inner world, you will find yourself in the realm of the unconscious where darkness predominates. Darkness can sometimes seem chillingly empty, but really it is always pregnant with the germ of new life. The difficult feelings you encounter while mothering can be painful, but they are not to be avoided. It is in this darkness that new things grow. It is darkness that gives rise to transformation.

A MAP FOR OUR JOURNEY

What might we expect from a journey down the well? We have a map available to us in the form of a fairy tale. "The Two Caskets" will serve as our guide for the journey down the well to find the secret wellspring of meaning in the inner world. It features the universal motif of descent, sojourn, and return that characterizes female initiation. There are many such tales that tell about what happens to a woman who descends to the depths. Perhaps the oldest of these is the ancient Mesopotamian story of the goddess Inanna and her descent to the underworld to visit her dark sister Ereshkigal. This and other such stories express a deep truth about the nature of a woman's psychological development that still applies today. "The Two Caskets" will prepare us for the journey we will take in the following pages of this book. It will show us what we might expect when we are cast down the well, what attitude we must take when we are at the bottom of the well, and the treasures we might gain upon our return. This is the first story to tell in the motherhood journey because, as mothers, we will be cast down the well over and over again.

 ## THE TWO CASKETS

Once there was a woman who had a daughter who was coarse, lazy, and rude, whom she loved and pampered. She also had a stepdaughter who was lovely, kind, and gracious, whom she treated worse than a servant. The woman hated her stepdaughter and wanted to find a way to get rid of her. One day, she had both daughters sit at the edge of the well and spin, warning them that the one whose thread broke first would be thrown to the bottom.

She gave her own daughter the finest flax so that it spun smoothly and without breaking. She gave her stepdaughter coarse stuff that quickly broke. Then the woman grabbed her stepdaughter by the shoulders and cast her down the well.

"And that is the end of you!" she said. But she was wrong, for it was only the beginning.

At the end of her fall, the girl found herself in a beautiful land. She walked for a while until she came upon a rickety old fence, overgrown with vines. "Please don't step on me!" said the fence. So the girl took care to jump over it. Next, she came to an oven full of bread. The oven told her she could eat as much as she liked but begged her not to hurt it. The girl ate one loaf, thanked the oven for its bread, and carefully closed its door. After walking for some distance, she happened upon a cow with a bucket hanging on its horns. It told the girl she was welcome to milk it and drink but asked the girl not to hurt it or spill the milk. The girl carefully milked the cow, drank her fill, and then hung the bucket back up without spilling.

At last, she came to a little house where an old woman lived. The woman bade her come in and asked her to comb her hair. The girl graciously combed the old woman's long, white hair, so the old woman gave her a job tending her cows. She took good care of the cows. When hungry cats came to the barn, the girl gave them milk. When hungry sparrows came, the girl gave them corn.

After the girl had been caring for the cows for some time, the old woman summoned her. "You have served me well," she said. "But now I have other tasks for you." She gave the girl a sieve and told her to fetch water with it. The girl was near tears at being given such an impossible task, but the birds that she had fed with the corn came and told her to stop up the sieve with ashes. The girl did so, and triumphantly carried water to the old woman as she had asked.

The old woman seemed surprised and set the girl another task. This time, she was to wash some black wool until it turned white and some white wool until it turned black. Again the girl was distraught and near tears, until the birds came and told her to face east to turn the black wool white and to face west to turn the white wool black. Once again, the old woman seemed surprised and even a little irritated at her success.

"I will set you one last task," she said. She told the girl to weave the wool into a robe as smooth as a king's and to do this by sunset, but the skeins tangled and broke each time, and the girl had no success. The cats to whom she had given milk came and wove it for her, and by sunset, the robe was finished, as perfect as can be.

"Because you have been so industrious," said the old woman, "I will let you choose a casket to take with you back to your home." She showed her to an attic filled with beautiful caskets. The girl considered each one, but the cats came and told her to take the plain black one.

Back at home, her stepmother was not happy to see her. But when the girl opened the little black casket, gold and jewels cascaded out, filling the henhouse the girl had been given as lodging.

Seeing this, the stepmother wanted her own daughter to get such riches. She had her sit by the well and spin, and then threw her down the well when her flax broke. The lazy girl proceeded as her sister had done, but she was rude to the fence, the oven, and the cow, and she worked very poorly on the farm. Because she was not kind to the birds and the cats, they did not help her with the tasks set to her by the old woman. At the end of her service, the lazy girl was given her choice of caskets in the attic, like her sister. Instead of choosing the small, plain, black casket, she chose a large red one, imagining that it would contain many more riches than the tiny one her sister had brought back. When she got home and opened her casket, however, fire burst out and burned her and her mother to death.

A SYMBOLIC UNDERSTANDING

When interpreting a fairy tale psychologically, we start with the assumption that all elements in the tale are aspects of a single psyche. Therefore, the stepmother, the cows, the old woman, and the well are all part of the psyche of the heroine and the story shows us possible ways these elements can interrelate. The two sisters, so opposite in their natures, can be understood to be different aspects of one personality. No one is good and virtuous and patient all the time. Some days we are the kind sister, and other days we are the lazy, arrogant sister. We all have both within us.

At the beginning of the tale, the kind sister is at the mercy of her cruel stepmother. Psychologically, this is an image of being oppressed by an inner critical voice that berates you and keeps your confidence low. It is no accident that this role is played in the tale by the stepmother. Often in the psyche of a woman, the inner voice that criticizes is the internalized voice of our actual mother, especially if our mother was critical and disparaging.

When we are oppressed by a constant inner stream of negative faultfinding, it is difficult to find an unbroken thread in things. We begin something—a project, a thought, a sentence—but we get pulled up and cut short by the inner critic. One of my patients, Caroline, loves to take books out of the library. She is an intelligent woman with a lively, curious mind, and she gets excited by the ideas contained in these books. However, she often finds that she does not read the books she checks out. They sit by her bedside, and when she sees them, a harshly judgmental voice tells her she has no business pursuing any of these interests as they are impractical, and she probably wouldn't understand them anyway. This inner voice is very similar to the discouraging way her mother and father would talk to her as a child. In this way, Caroline's thread through life breaks continually, and she finds she cannot sustain an interest in anything long enough to make progress.

Just imagine what it would feel like to sit on the edge of a well and try to do any sort of work that requires careful attention. You wouldn't be able to relax or give your work your full concentration. You would constantly feel "on edge," as it were, with the threat of falling in ever present. Many of us live in just this way, always balancing ourselves precariously on the edge of our dark moods, expending a great deal of emotional energy to avoid tipping over and falling into them. While we may successfully stay on the surface and evade the plunge into the depths, such a strategy can exhaust and deplete us, making it difficult for us to engage in life fully.

When life throws you down the well, it is always a painful, frightening, and disorienting experience. What will make the difference as to whether you return with the treasure or the curse has to do with the approach that you take toward the unconscious—the marvelous land at the bottom of the well.

Always with the unconscious, it is necessary to have the correct attitude. If you face the unconscious with arrogance, clinging adamantly to an ego attitude that insists on having its own way, you are likely to meet with the destructive side of the unconscious. When you behave toward your inner life like the lazy sister, disregarding promptings from the unconscious and expecting to be given something for nothing, you will find that plans go awry and energy dries up. You are thwarted at every turn and feel you cannot trust life.

If you approach the unconscious like the kind sister, if you are willing to engage it with openness and curiosity no matter how strange or worthless it seems, then the world opens up, little by little. We treat our dreams with care, no matter how silly or absurd they seem. We attend to the faint stirrings of intuition. We notice what our bodies have to say on matters. If we live in this way, we will be in right relationship with our unconscious. Like the kind sister, we will be serving the old woman well and can expect to be richly rewarded.

UNIVERSAL THEMES

Fairy tales and myths are filled with images that convey universal themes that recur throughout time and across cultures. The witch, the wise old man, and the mother are just a few examples of such images. Jung used the term "archetype" to describe these fundamental patterns that are inborn and part of our common psychological heritage. They exist in all of us. Archetypes are the universal innate forms that structure our psychological life. Though they can be imaged in a variety of ways, the symbolic taproot of these energies always goes down to the same deep source. The archetypes are ancient and relate to our most profound instinctual wisdom. When we encounter them, they often provoke strong emotions.

The well is an example of an archetypal image, symbolizing a descent into the depths that is both frightening and potentially renewing. The well is the central metaphor in our tale—and in this book. Wells are often associated with the feminine and are sacred to the goddess in many cultures. When we partake of the waters of the well, we are restored to the sacred feminine within. Going down the well, therefore, is an image of initiation into the feminine depths of the psyche. Mothering can be like being thrown down a deep well. Like any initiatory experience, such a journey forces you to surrender control and descend into your depths where a confrontation with your soul awaits you. If borne with humility, curiosity, and openheartedness, such an experience has the potential to be transformative—to enlarge our sense of who we are, to clarify our place in the great arc and sweep of time, and to affirm our belonging to the cosmos.

When you go down the well, you will encounter the archetypal sacred feminine, which the old woman certainly is. This old woman lives in you, and you will meet her on your motherhood journey. Like all archetypes, the old woman has two aspects. She can be life-giving and creative, or punishing and destructive. Other versions of this tale tell us more about the mysterious dual nature of the old woman. In one version, the old woman makes it snow on Earth when she shakes out her feather bed, making it clear that she is none other than a primordial nature goddess. In other versions, her weird grotesqueness is emphasized. She has strangely large teeth, her hair is full of lice, or she is able to remove and replace her head at will. Always she is ambivalent, capable of bestowing great riches but also of invoking great destructive powers. This is ever the nature of the energies that form the basis of psychic life. You will likely encounter her in both of her aspects as you mother.

Two other archetypal images are particularly prominent in this story and therefore merit a bit more exploration. Spinning and weaving appear as key motifs throughout this tale. These humble activities carry enormous symbolic meaning. In Greek and Norse mythology, the Fates who control people's lives are spinners and weavers. The prominence of spinning and weaving in this tale lets us know that it treats the fundamental aspects of how we create the fabric of our fate through the myriad daily choices we make.

The cow is another image that appears in multiple places in the tale. The cow is a picture of the nourishing, maternal aspects of the unconscious. In Norse and Egyptian mythologies, the cow was associated with human creation, and the cow is sacred in Hinduism. The importance of the cow in this tale emphasizes that the gentle, life-giving nature of the sacred feminine exists alongside the strange and frightening aspect. It is a reminder that we can always find renewing nourishment within. Even when you encounter the frightening or strange aspect of the old woman, remember that the gentle cow, too, is part of you and is present.

FEMININE INITIATION

In essence, "The Two Caskets" and the many related tales of a descent into the underworld where the heroine encounters a sometimes-threatening female deity are images of feminine initiation. These tales map out an ancient archetypal pattern faced by women the world over since the dawn of human consciousness. The journey involves three distinct stages; descent, sojourn, and return. These are the same stages found in initiation rites the world over, in which the initiate must first separate from his family and tribe, then undergo an ordeal before finally returning to family and tribe with a new status. Initiation rites are meant to set us on our path, to open our hearts to the deep, mysterious purpose inherent in us at birth.

Today, few of us participate in formal rituals of initiation. Even without these, however, life initiates us. An initiatory life event is that which cracks us open, shakes us out of our familiar tread, and challenges us to reconsolidate a sense of ourselves along new, more expansive lines. Whether we are consciously aware of it or not, we are all repeatedly faced with chances to become initiated into our life's secret purpose. Life presents us with myriad opportunities to journey down the well and prove ourselves for the chance to return with the treasure of greater psychological wholeness. Any challenging experience has the potential to cast us into our own depths, but motherhood may be the life experience most effective at doing so.

Questions for Reflection for
Journey to the Source

1. Initiations always involve an ordeal that tests us, breaks us open, and reveals to us our destiny. Even if we don't go through formal rites of initiation, life will initiate us. What in your life has served as an initiation?

2. Imagine you are the stepmother who hates her stepdaughter so much that she is always looking for ways to get rid of her. Is there anything in your life that you have such feelings toward? What in your life do you sometimes wish you could throw down a well? Perhaps there is an aspect of yourself that you despise this much? Are there times you treat a part of yourself worse than a servant?

3. The kind daughter must sit at the edge of the well and try to spin coarse flax, which breaks easily. Where in your life are you in a precarious situation such as this? Where have you been set an impossible task?

4. As the kind girl tries to spin, the thread keeps breaking. Sometimes we try and try to get things going in some aspect of our lives without success. When in your life was this true for you?

5. The kind daughter is thrown into the dark depths without warning. This must have been very frightening. She likely did not know whether she would survive the fall, and she certainly didn't know what awaited her at the bottom. When in your life have you faced a terrifying unknown?

6. When have you treated your inner life like the kind daughter? Perhaps you allowed yourself to rest when you felt tired or otherwise listened to what your body was trying to tell you. Maybe you wrote down your dreams or heeded your intuition.

7. When have you treated your inner life like the lazy daughter? Maybe you ignored messages from your unconscious about times when you felt tired or depleted and forced yourself to push through anyway. Maybe you took for granted the gifts of the unconscious, such as dreams or moods.

8. Which casket have you chosen? Describe a time recently when you have chosen the equivalent of the small, black casket. Maybe you chose something that was less prestigious or showy but ultimately more gratifying. When in your life have you chosen the equivalent of the flashy red casket—something that was very impressive in a superficial way but destructive to your happiness or well-being in the end?

PART I

DOWN THE WELL

CHAPTER 1

Losing Freedom

Unless one accepts one's fate . . . there is no individuation;
one remains a mere accident, a mortal nothing.

C. G. JUNG

AS QUOTED IN *THE WAY OF INDIVIDUATION*

To be thrown down the well is to find yourself at the mercy of inner and outer forces beyond your conscious control. Above all, such a descent will initially involve multiple losses, including the loss of freedom, the loss of control, and even the loss of yourself. There are many ways in which we, as mothers, will be cast down the well. Finding our way back can be more difficult for some of us than for others, depending on the situation, the nature of our relationship with our child, and how we were parented. We all reach adulthood having sustained some injury to our developing sense of self. These wounds will surface in new ways when we become parents, creating unique challenges for us but also offering us new opportunities to heal them. If you have a shaky sense of self, you might experience motherhood as a threat to what little freedom and autonomy you have been able to claim. Your journey down the well will likely be painful and fraught, but it will also invite the possibility of connecting deeply with your ground of being.

Being raised by a narcissistic parent can create a wound that makes mothering particularly difficult. If you had parents who required that you met their needs or helped them regulate their feelings about themselves by mirroring them, you may be especially prone to having a weak sense of self. Growing up in this way, you will likely arrive in adulthood with very little sense of who you are and what matters to you. You may have a wounded sense of whether you deserve to have your feelings or whether you can ask for what you need. You will find it hard to commit to anything—including your own life. If you have not been taught to protect and stand up for yourself, motherhood can easily overwhelm you, causing you to feel confined.

Our first intimation that motherhood has cast us down the well may be an experience of being trapped—our freedom curtailed, our options limited. If we haven't had a chance to consolidate a sense of who we are before becoming a mother, this enforced limitation can be experienced as a bitter constraint. A woman might feel depleted by the constant demands of parenthood. She may have trouble setting boundaries or asking for help and may therefore come to feel resentful of her children.

If you were unmothered because of a physically or emotionally unavailable mom, this can leave you with unresolved issues when it comes time for you to parent. In this case, your mothering journey will likely take you through a dark passage. Being a mother may reawaken devastating feelings of abandonment and isolation. When old painful emotions resurface, the journey will be difficult. But trust that these wounds are being brought into awareness again so that you can have the opportunity to heal them. Being open to your inner world, even when this is painful, always offers the possibility of renewal.

ABDUCTED AND IMPRISONED

Constance entered treatment with me shortly after the birth of her first child. She had left her job as a paralegal at a law firm after the baby came, and she felt isolated and full of despair about her marriage. "I feel trapped," she said. "I just want to run away."

Constance had never had the chance to know herself or discover what she liked. She had never been able to find an authentic "yes" because she had never been given permission to say an authentic "no." Raised in a wealthy Boston family, Constance grew up in privilege and comfort. Her mother, however, was brittle with many unmet narcissistic needs. From very early on, Constance's mother required that Constance meet those needs.

For example, Constance's mother had gone to great lengths to plan an elaborate christening. She was hosting the luncheon at an exclusive club downtown, and she had engaged the very best catering company in Boston. Family and friends from all over were flying in for the occasion. The day of the christening, however, three-month-old Constance awoke with a fever. Though she was listless and quite obviously sick, her mother dosed her with acetaminophen and proceeded to dress her in the expensive christening gown she had special ordered. Rather than bringing her sick baby home directly after the church service, Constance's mother kept her at the luncheon the entire afternoon. The story has entered family lore, with her mother insisting that she had no idea how sick Constance was because she never even cried once that day. Constance has photographs of herself from the party, glassy-eyed, red-cheeked, being held and repeatedly photographed by differing combinations of visiting family. Two days later, she was admitted to the hospital with a respiratory infection. She didn't come home for several days.

As Constance grew up, she was expected to be compliant and attractive. Her mother was thin and always dieting. Constance, however, was a plump child who became a heavy adolescent. Constance recalled with pain the weight-loss camps, clinics, and doctors that her mother took her to through middle school and high school. She felt she was letting her mother down by not being pretty and slender enough. Constance brought photographs of herself as a child to one of our sessions, and I got to see her when she was "fat." In one photograph, twelve-year-old Constance stands with a cousin at the beach. The two girls are wearing bathing suits. Constance looks at the camera with a smile that is hesitant, a little unsure. She is a bit heavy, and this is accentuated by the juxtaposition with her cousin, who is all giraffe legs and spindly arms, hips jutting out of her suit. But twelve-year-old Constance is hardly fat. I took in the photo, the tentative smile, the question in her eyes. I knew that, by this time, she had already begun "dieting" at her mother's insistence.

By the time she had grown to adulthood, Constance was well adapted to sensing and meeting the needs of others around her. Before becoming a mother, Constance navigated her life with a key strategy she had been taught to rely on in order to survive her childhood with her narcissistic mother: she complied with what the other person wanted. Almost as soon as she and Charles started dating, he began aggressively pushing for them to get married. Constance recalls that she wasn't even sure what her feelings were about him at the time. She felt swept along by his insistence, and she never got her feet under her to take a firm stand to slow things down. Within two years, they were married with a baby on the way.

Constance loved her son and was an attentive and attached parent. But he was a difficult baby who had special medical needs and required a great deal of care and monitoring. Because she had never authentically chosen to be married or pregnant, it was difficult for Constance to weather the disappointments and challenges in marriage and motherhood. She had only just begun to entertain possibilities for herself when her son came along, seemingly taking away opportunities for growth and exploration that she was only starting to imagine.

A fairy tale from Scotland tells us about the psychology of such a woman who has no firm sense of self. "The Selkie Bride" is the story of a woman for whom marriage and motherhood were abduction and imprisonment.

THE SELKIE BRIDE

Once, a poor farmer came upon three beautiful maidens singing in the moonlight by the ocean on midsummer. Enchanted, he watched from the shadows, but when he took a step toward them, they started, quickly pulled on their gray garments, and slipped into the water.

The farmer was stricken, for he had fallen in love with the beautiful maidens and couldn't stop thinking of how he wanted one to be his wife. At last, he consulted a wise woman, who told him that the maidens were selkies, beings who live as seals beneath the water but are also capable of shedding their seal skin to walk on land as people. She advised him how he could trap and hold a selkie for his own.

At the next midsummer, when he knew the selkie maidens would again appear, the farmer waited in hiding. He watched them emerge and remove their gray seal skins. When he saw his chance, he rushed out from the shadows and grabbed one of the skins. Alarmed, the three selkie maidens made for their skins. Two slipped into the water, but the third looked about, distressed. Her sisters called to her from the waves, but the lone maiden stood shivering, naked and alone on the shore, looking out to sea. The farmer came to her, gently covered her with his coat, and led her back to his little farm, explaining that he promised to be a good and kind husband to her.

From that day, they lived together as man and wife, and the farmer was as good as his word, working hard to provide for his new little family. As the wise woman had advised, he had carefully hidden away the skin behind a loose brick, and he took it out secretly once a year to oil it and to make sure it was in good repair. The selkie bride dutifully kept house for her husband. In time, she gave birth to fine children, each of whom had their mother's soulful brown eyes. However, she often went to the beach at twilight, where she would gaze wistfully out to sea. And though she loved her children dearly, they never saw her smile.

One day, her youngest boy came to her and asked why his father kept an old skin behind a loose brick. The selkie started, her eyes alight. Kneeling down, she asked her son to show her. When once she had retrieved the skin, she embraced her son warmly, and then with nary a backward glance, she ran down to the shore and was never seen again.

Selkie stories feature beautiful shape-shifting women abducted against their will by human men. They are full of sadness and longing. Psychologically, they illustrate what happens to a woman when she has never had the chance to freely make her own choices about how to live her life. As a result, commitment is experienced as an intolerable sacrifice of her freedom, and she longs to run away, imagining that escape will protect her fragile selfhood.

The theft of the skin is often interpreted as an image of enforced subservience of the woman, and this is indeed one way we can understand it. In order to meet traditional expectations of marriage and motherhood, a woman is often required to cut herself off from that part of her that is a wild creature of the depths. According to this understanding, there is no genuine solution to this dilemma. The loss of a woman's freedom is inevitable, tragic, and unredeemed. If this version of the tale is our truth—as I believe it may be, sadly, for some—then motherhood will not be an experience of growth but a stunting of it. Living in the balance between asserting our needs and desires and sacrificing these in service to something larger will require resilience and creativity. Supportive partners, families, workplaces, and societal norms can make all the difference.

THE REWARDS OF SACRIFICE

There is another way to understand the theft of the skin. A key developmental task of growing up involves sacrificing our youthful experience of endless potential for the limitation and fixity of adulthood. When we are young and have not yet made a serious commitment to a partner, a child, or a career, all possibilities remain hypothetically open to us. At some point, we will be asked to sacrifice unlimited potential for lived reality. Becoming a mother is often the point at which many of us face this sacrifice, and it is just at this point in her development that the selkie has difficulty.

If we make this sacrifice, we become changed. We grow in ways that may be surprising even to ourselves. If we cannot make the required sacrifice, however, we may continue to be the eternal girl, refusing to give up youthful things in spite of the outward appearance of adulthood. In the psyche, when we cannot let something die, the result is that we cannot fully live.

In order to become firmly planted in your unique life, you must sacrifice unlimited potential for the manifested reality of ordinary fate. When you do so, you accept the necessity of being "pinned down, of entering space and time completely, and of being the specific human being that one is,"[1] to use the language of Jungian analyst

Marie-Louise von Franz. This is a sacrifice that must be made in order to embrace maturity.

The seal skin is that which keeps open the option of a return to life in the open waters. It may represent a vital time in a young woman's life when she has unrestrained freedom to engage in experimentation and focus only on herself. However, it is also right that, at some point, such a skin be laid aside to make room for a new sort of life, one that is in the interest of serving a greater purpose, be it a relationship, a career, or the care of a child. When we are determined to cling to our youthful life at any cost, the theft of our seal skin will be experienced as a terrible violation, when in fact it may be the thing that creates an opportunity for growth.

If we consider the tale psychologically, the farmer who would like to keep the selkie tethered to the fixed form of a woman is an *inner* energy. (Recall that we are assuming that everyone in the tale represents a part of a single psyche.) For someone with selkie psychology, the farmer would represent that part of the personality that would like to settle down to a rather ordinary life. Since he is a small farmer, we can see that this part of the psyche is indeed very earthy and grounded, unlike the slippery, watery selkie. Interpreting the tale this way keeps things wonderfully ambivalent. Is the farmer's energy oppressive? Or might he also be a positive, grounding impulse that could open the way to new life and new growth?

LOSING OUR SKIN

According to one understanding of the story, the selkie is presented with an opportunity to grow by becoming more grounded, but ultimately she is not able to do so. There are intimations at the beginning of the story that her sense of self is too weak for her to be able to undergo the required transformation. The selkie has neither name nor a unique identity. The farmer grabs a skin indiscriminately, without having singled out an individual object of affection. The heroine is never differentiated from the other selkies. Even after all her time on land, the selkie bride doesn't manage to consolidate an individual personality and is easily subsumed back into the watery unconscious once there is no longer anything to hold her on dry land.

A woman manifesting this pattern may not have had a chance to develop her unique tastes and preferences. She may not have a strong sense of self and may not have separated psychologically from her parents. A selkie woman has grown up without ever having had permission to disappoint or be unpleasant. Without the secure knowledge that we will be loved and accepted even when we disagree or are disagreeable, we cannot learn who we genuinely are and what truly matters to us. We find it unbearably uncomfortable to experience conflict or anger with a loved one. Therefore we find ourselves subject to the tyranny of others' wishes, needs, and demands, since we are not armed with the ability to say no or assert our needs. In this unprotected and supremely vulnerable state, it is easy for another to rob us of our self, to steal away the skin of our fragile identity.

Constance had never been helped to feel and assert her authentic reactions. Sensitive, intuitive, and introverted, Constance found it difficult to interact with anyone—friends, family, or even shopkeepers—without tuning in to that person's needs and finding a way to meet them. This was, understandably, incredibly taxing and exhausting. She found that only when she was alone could she be herself. When Constance was with others, she had to be "nice" at all times and shape-shift herself into a form that would meet the other person's expectations. She therefore spent a great deal of time cut off from her essence. In this state, she became increasingly depleted and depressed.

When you don't know your own needs or don't feel entitled to speak up for them, you run the risk of being captured by those who make demands on you. When Constance met Charles, she was so busy unconsciously tuning in to his needs and preferences that she barely had time to be aware of her feelings for him. Because of this, she found herself "abducted" into the relationship before she had a chance to experiment with the forms her life could take; before she had fully learned who she was so that she might make a conscious choice.

Often, selkie women are those who have had had narcissistic mothers who themselves needed to be mirrored and emotionally cared for by their daughters. The actor Brooke Shields is an example of a selkie woman, and she has written about her complicated relationship with her mother, Teri. Teri was fiercely protective of her daughter while also enmeshed with her. In her memoir about her mother, Shields catalogs the many ways in which she cared emotionally for the fragile, alcoholic Teri. In one example, Shields discusses how difficult it was for her to consummate her first sexual relationship with her college boyfriend because having sex felt as though it would be an act of separating from her mother, and because she had no clear sense of what she, herself, wanted. She could not attune to her authentic preferences about whether or not to lose her virginity with her boyfriend because her mother loomed so large in her psyche. "Even when Mom wasn't around, I felt as if she was watching,"[2] writes Shields.

Those who have had to meet the emotional needs of their parents like Constance or Brooke Shields have been forced to capitulate on their sense of truth, and therefore they have lost—or never gained—the sense of belonging to themselves. Commitment cannot be voluntary for a person with selkie psychology because she does not truly belong to herself, and so she cannot give herself to anything or anyone else. Therefore commitments such as marriage or children feel like enforced constraint. When such a woman has a child, motherhood can be experienced as a devastating loss of options, entrapment in a fixed form not consciously chosen.

PROVISIONAL COMMITMENT

The selkie's seal skin tucked behind a loose brick is an image of a provisional commitment. The tie to the old life has not been completely severed. The farmer part of the psyche renews and replenishes this secret, hidden attachment to the old carefree life—a metaphor for the tentative, ambivalent commitment this psyche has to the new life. Animal bride (or bridegroom) tales are a common motif and occur all over the world. In some, the human captor must quickly burn the animal skin of his bride. While this might sound violent and oppressive, often these tales end happily. Since burning is a complete chemical transformation of a substance from one thing into something entirely different, a story in which the skin has been burned can be understood psychologically to mean that the new (human) identity has been fully integrated. The shape-shifting animal has been authentically transformed. Because the old life has been sacrificed in the fires of transformation, the new life can be fully lived and embraced.

Like the selkie, Constance had never quite committed to her marriage. When tensions between her and her husband grew, the idea of leaving was always there in the background, like the seal skin hidden behind the brick. And she was very reluctant to give it up. Several times, things escalated to the point where she and her husband were ready to seek couples therapy, but each time, it was Constance who demurred. As she and I explored why this was, we came to understand that making that level of commitment to her marriage—of really trying to work out some of the issues that plagued them—was very threatening to Constance. Doing this work would have been like burning the seal skin, and then she wouldn't have been able to flee back to the water. Her retreat would have been cut off. The thought that she could always leave had made her situation more bearable for her.

THE HIDDEN BENEFITS OF BEING A SELKIE

There is a hidden benefit to being a selkie woman. Like the fairy-tale heroine, women who haven't learned who they are yet can be shapeshifters, slipping between different forms depending on what they sense is required of them. This quality can be particularly attractive to men, who can project onto these women whatever qualities they desire to see, and the selkie women will unconsciously oblige them by carrying those projections. Because the selkie woman remains open to becoming whatever those around her need her to be, she never has to face the limitation inherent in consolidating a firm and enduring sense of self. She can remain fluid, able at any moment to return to the sea of endless possibility.

A selkie woman can remain an "eternal girl," an archetype that Jung dubbed the *puella*. Such a woman may flit through existence enjoying the lifestyle of a younger person even as she ages. Such a life can be exciting, but it also comes at a cost. Julie was forty years old when she first came to see me, but her short skirt, knee-high boots, and lacy top seemed more appropriate to someone half her age.

Petite, pretty, and demure, she confessed during our work together that she had never reconciled herself to her marriage to Pete, who was steady but rather dull. The couple had married when they were both twenty-three, but they had not been physically intimate for many years. Instead, Julie pursued affairs with exciting men who always disappointed her when they refused to commit. Without such a commitment from a lover, Julie did not feel capable of giving up the stability offered by her marriage. Julie had not yet come to terms with the need to let go of endless possibility. By insisting on leaving all of her options open, she was living out a girlish pattern. Although she enjoyed the fun and excitement of late nights out and new lovers, she was not changing or developing.

Allowing ourselves to let go of freedom and embrace the ordinary fate is a kind of fall from grace, a small tragedy. With her fantasies of flight always in the back of her mind, Constance had an illusion of there being unlimited potential. When she contemplated truly committing to her current life, she was often overwhelmed by a panicky sense of claustrophobia. To do so would mean coming to terms with life being finite and flawed, something less than she might have imagined for herself. On the other hand, it would mean that she had finally become real, made up of solid stuff, however imperfect.

Brooke Shields also experienced the commitment demanded by motherhood as problematic. In her brave memoir of postpartum depression, she details the collapse she experienced after her daughter's birth. Having grown up taking care of her mother and deferring to her mother's opinion, she was easily overwhelmed by the demands of caring for an infant. Since she had been made responsible her whole life for her alcoholic mother, it isn't surprising that she felt engulfed and resentful when she found herself responsible for this new little being.

Selkie women dream of running away. Shields's fantasies of escape are typical for women with selkie psychology. She admits that she "spent time fantasizing about disappearing forever."[3] One of the most striking aspects of the fairy tale is the ease with which the mother leaves her children. We see that for the many long years she has lived on land, she has never stopped yearning to return to the sea. She has always been waiting for just such an opportunity. Poignantly, we realize that she has never fully been attached.

Running away—from children, commitments, places—appears as a magical solution when we have never fully consolidated a strong sense of self. When Constance felt emotionally abandoned by her husband during the first difficult year of her son's life, she fell immediately into mute despair. Expressing her need for more attuned interaction with him was far more terrifying than the thought of numbly soldiering on. Caught between these two places—being alone and sad within the relationship on the one hand, and risking the conflict that often comes with taking a stand on the other—Constance found no satisfactory solution other than to run. She fantasized about leaving her husband and child behind and going off to live on her own out West. Flight seemed the only possible answer to her dilemma. She could not imagine that there might be a way to remain in the relationship and be authentic to the nascent sense of self that was trying to get born.

Ultimately, "The Selkie Bride" is a story of a failed initiation. The mother in the tale has been presented with a very difficult challenge of growing down into the authentic soil of herself and joining fully with the inner farmer energy, but she has no idea how to do that. Like a plant that has fallen on shallow soil so that its roots cannot grow deep, a selkie woman easily gets washed away, blown over with even a moderate wind. Her return to the sea and her seal form imply that she has become less conscious, going back to the water and to the less differentiated seal way of being. At the end of the tale, she has not changed but has merely returned untransformed to her initial state. In this sense, the selkie is very much like the lazy daughter who went down the well in "The Two Caskets." She isn't able to make the required sacrifice that will lead to transformation and growth.

If life's task is to grow into the person we were meant to be, then the selkie woman has her work cut out for her. Becoming a mother provides a new opportunity for a selkie to learn what truly matters for her. It can be the catalyst for separating from her parents and beginning to know her truth. Motherhood can be an opportunity for a selkie woman to differentiate her needs from the wants of others, to take a stand, and to make a commitment to herself. What does it look like when we are able to meet the challenge and go through the required transformation so that we return with the treasure? To answer this question, we can look to another fairy tale about shape-shifting maidens.

THE SWAN MAIDEN

There was once a hunter who came to a lake near sunset one evening. As he watched, he saw seven swans descend to land on the water. Reaching the bank, they one by one climbed out of the water, shed their feathered swan skins, and transformed into beautiful maidens. The loveliest among them, however, was the youngest. The hunter watched entranced, but he had not lost his wits. Carefully, he crept toward them as silently as he could until he was just close enough to grab the feathered garment of the smallest and youngest swan maiden. The maidens started in fright. Each one quickly donned her swan robe and flew off into the sky save the youngest, who huddled alone, covering her nakedness as best she could. The hunter covered her with his cloak and led her back to his home, where she became his wife.

The couple lived together many years contentedly and had two children, a boy and a girl. Their mother loved them with all of her heart. One day, the children were playing hide-and-seek together when the girl found a dusty feathered robe tucked in the corner of the attic. Curious, she took it to her mother. The mother took her daughter by her shoulders and looked into her eyes. "Tell your father that if he wishes to see me again, he must find me in the land east of the sun and west of the moon." Then she donned her feathered robe and flew away.

When her husband came home and heard what had happened, he set out immediately, venturing far and wide. He had to ask many times for help finding this faraway place, consulting the King of the Beasts, the King of the Birds, and the King of the Fishes. Along the way, two quarreling brothers asked his help to settle a dispute about their inheritance, which consisted of a magic hat that rendered the wearer invisible and magic shoes that transported the wearer wherever he wished. The hunter tricked the brothers, taking the items for himself and using them to come at last to the Crystal Mountain, where his wife was living.

The hunter approached the King of the Crystal Mountain and explained that he was the husband of the king's youngest daughter, and he had come to bring her home. Then the king said, "If you can tell her from her sisters, then I know that what you say is true."

He called his seven daughters to him, and there they all were! They were wearing their feathered gowns, and each looked just the same, as similar to one another as one swan to another.

But the hunter wasn't dismayed. "If I may look at each of their hands, I will know my wife for sure," he said to himself, for she had sewn the little clothes for her children, and the forefinger of her right hand had the marks of the needle. When he had taken the hand of each of the swan maidens, he did indeed soon find his wife. The King of the Crystal Mountain gave the couple many rich gifts and sent them on their way. They soon were home again with their children, where they lived happily ever after for the remainder of their days.

Swan maiden stories appear at first glance to be very similar to selkie stories, but right away, there are important differences. Notably, most selkie stories have the farmer grabbing a seal skin randomly, hoping to capture any one of the selkie maidens. We saw that this lack of individuality presaged the selkie's ultimate failure to consolidate an unique identity. In the swan maiden tale, the hunter spies out the swan skin of the youngest and prettiest and makes a point of selecting that skin. This theme repeats itself at the climax of the tale when the hunter must once again select his wife from among the other swans. The swan maiden, therefore, begins the tale with a nascent sense of her own individuality. She is seen and recognized right from the beginning as someone unique and special. This will be developed and triumphantly consolidated by the end of the tale.

YOU ARE UNIQUE—AND ORDINARY

An important theme of this story involves the idea of individuality. Not coincidentally, learning who we are in our particularity is a critical part of becoming the person we were meant to be. To develop a stronger sense of self, a woman needs to inhabit the unique preferences and quirks that make her who she is. Rather than going along with what others want, she gives voice to her own likes and dislikes. The fairy tale shows us that mothering can be an experience that gives rise to a unique sense of self. The swan maiden's fingers have been marked by the needle used to make clothes for her children. The daily challenges of mothering do indeed leave their scars, marking a woman as an individual with a unique history. Long after she is dead, a mother's bones will show that she has borne a child. Motherhood marks us forever.

This is where we see the significance of the swan maiden and her calloused fingers. By giving herself over to the ordinary fate of motherhood with its endless menial tasks, she has become a unique, solid individual. She has left behind the realm of endless possibility where one doesn't grow up and nothing is risked, and embraced the opportunity to descend into the sweet center of her life in a fully embodied way.

Once she has been marked by motherhood, the swan maiden is no longer indistinguishable from her sisters. In her daily toil on behalf of her children, she has become herself uniquely. Like the kind daughter in "The Two Caskets" who descended to the depths with the appropriate attitude and made the sacrifice required for transformation, the swan maiden has descended from her lofty heights as a swan into an embodied woman. Even though she exhibits ambivalence about her new life in the middle of the tale, by the end of the story she has sacrificed her fantasies of eternal youth and come to terms with her ordinariness. To do as the swan maiden does requires us to trade in an exciting but inflated and unrealistic sense of endless possibility for an experience of ourselves sturdily grounded in our authenticity.

Embracing life requires that you gracefully accept your ordinary, human fate. The Skin Horse from the classic children's story *The Velveteen Rabbit* knows that when we relinquish the inflation of perfection and claim our singular ordinariness, we gain something priceless.

You become. It takes a long time. That's why it doesn't happen often to people who break easily, or have sharp edges, or who have to be carefully kept. Generally, by the time you are Real, most of your hair has been loved off, and your eyes drop out and you get loose in your joints and very shabby. But these things don't matter at all, because once you are Real, you can't be ugly, except to people who don't understand.[4]

The scars of the swan maiden and the bare patches of the Skin Horse are beautiful because they are a testament to a unique journey, a mark of having lived and loved.

LISTENING TO OURSELVES

Developing a sense of a unique self will require us to listen to ourselves. Brooke Shields found that becoming a mother helped her to hear and eventually listen to her instincts, intuitions, and opinions. She was able to differentiate herself from her mother and hear what she herself authentically desired.

It took me a while and a great deal of painful trial and error to emotionally free myself from my mother and to have faith in my own convictions. . . . I had experienced a taste of autonomy at college by exercising my mind, but it was limited to my studies. It was not until much later that I began to form my own ideas and speak out based on my creative instincts. Motherhood, and the increasing confidence it afforded me, furthered this growth.

After I had Rowan, my inner voice became much more audible. It was a revelation to me that just because my opinions were different from my mother's (and other people's), it did not mean they were wrong. When it came to raising my own child, it was as if I got to start all over again, and this time I would follow my own instincts. This did not happen overnight; initially I had difficulty even finding my instincts because of the depression, but eventually my own solid beliefs and opinions surfaced.[5]

Once we are able to listen to our values and preferences, we will be better able to make a conscious commitment to them. However, as Shields points out, this process takes time and will likely involve setbacks.

Like the selkie, the swan maiden initially is unable to make a full commitment to her earthbound life. She seems content and settled with her life, yet some unfinished piece of business hangs forgotten in her psychic attic until this conflict is awakened by her growing daughter. So it is indeed often the case that when our children—perhaps especially our daughters—reach a stage of development in which they confront a challenge in their lives that we never managed to resolve fully on our own, old issues are reawakened for us. The feathered robe hanging in the attic is an image of the ways, little and big, that we may not have completely made peace with our lot in life. We may all have a few hidden impulses to fly away from our fate. We dream of escaping our ordinariness, and in this way we are not completely committed to ourselves and our life.

When I was eleven or twelve, just on the magical but perilous cusp of adolescence, I had an important friendship with a girl in my neighborhood. Her family was French, and both her parents spoke with an enchanting French accent. Everything about Celine's life appeared charmed to me—her mother's elegant style of dress, the European ski vacations they took, the food her mother prepared, and the sophisticated way her home was decorated. I was completely seduced by Celine and her family. My mother was a little wary of all of this European refinement, and especially of my fondness for it. I recall her pointedly noting my tendency to talk with Celine's mannerisms after I had spent time at her house.

Ultimately my friendship with Celine was one of an unrequited yearning to be accepted into a sphere that felt glamorous and sophisticated. My fraught desires to be accepted in this way had deep roots, as my mother often felt out of place as a Georgia farm girl in suburban Connecticut. This was indeed unfinished business.

When my daughter was around the same age that I was when I became friends with Celine, she too developed a sort of magical friendship with a girl who lived down the street. Olivia was a little bit older but much worldlier and more sophisticated. Both of her parents were writers—her father was a professor and poet, while her mother had written a well-received memoir. Olivia's mother was petite and stylish and looked unselfconsciously fantastic in whatever funky outfit she threw on. Their home was cleverly furnished with idiosyncratic collectibles, and they had frequent impromptu parties that were always attended by an eclectic group of local artists, academics, and intellectuals. I felt flattered to be included.

Olivia was charming, bright, and creative. In social groups, she was often the most sought-after child. She warmed to my daughter immediately, and the two of them created imaginary worlds together in their play. In truth, I became a bit spellbound, as I had years earlier with Celine's family. I was happy to turn my daughter over to this new friendship, allowing her to spend hours at a time at Olivia's house. Unlike my mother, I did not rein in my daughter's tendency to want to emulate Olivia, but, I am afraid, indirectly encouraged it. By doing so, I left my daughter exposed and unprotected from subtle pressures to be someone that she really wasn't. She started to return from time spent with Olivia sullen and withdrawn. It was only then that I realized what had happened and took steps to remedy the situation.

My daughter's friendship with Olivia reawakened for me this bit of unfinished business from my past. Feelings of inadequacy and longing to be someone that I wasn't—like the swan maiden's feathered robe—had been neatly tucked away for years but not entirely resolved. This left me susceptible to giving myself—and my daughter—over to this longed-for fantasy. In doing so, it was as if I had flown away, temporarily fleeing from my ground, and becoming caught in a flighty attempt to reach for something insubstantial and inauthentic.

Like the swan maiden, I had temporarily regressed to an earlier point in my development. In my case, this involved revisiting some painful, unresolved issues related to belonging and exclusion. In doing so, I had emotionally abandoned my daughter. It was a difficult lesson for me, but one that allowed me to work through earlier, unfinished business. When I saw my daughter's distress, I needed to do the hard work of admitting my part in the situation. I had to give up my fantasy of being in the glamorous "in" crowd and settle for being my rather pedestrian self, firmly rooted in my role as protector of my daughter's autonomy and sense of self. I chose to be real and ordinary, and in so doing, I returned to myself a little humbler but also a little wiser and stronger.

By facing the challenges of motherhood, a selkie woman may find that she can learn to know herself in her unique individuality. She can come to differentiate her needs for herself from the needs and expectations that others have of her. Her ability to stand up for and protect herself makes it possible for her to commit authentically to a child, a family, or a career. If you find that you are a bit of a selkie woman, motherhood may feel like an entrapment and a loss of freedom. But it will also be an opportunity to claim your unique ordinariness so that you have the opportunity to become the person you were meant to be. If things go well, selkie women become swan maidens. They meet the challenge of growing into the most authentic version of themselves, becoming transformed in the process.

Questions for Reflection for Losing Freedom

1. Both the selkie and the swan maiden have their skins stolen from them when they are unsuspecting and vulnerable. When has some important aspect of yourself been taken from you, perhaps leading you to feel trapped?

2. Where have you stolen your own skin? Maybe you committed to something uncomfortable that part of you didn't want to do. Maybe you let yourself be captured—by an idea, a role, a person, a job. If so, what might the hidden benefits be to being captured in this way? How was this an attempt to grow toward health?

3. What part of you is like the selkie—carefree and fluidly moving between different versions of yourself? What part of you is like the farmer—stable, earthy, and maybe a little boring and staid?

4. What secret part of yourself have you hidden away behind a loose brick or up in your psychic attic? What unresolved feelings keep you connected to the past and less available to your current life?

5. In what ways have you made only a provisional commitment to your life?

6. The hunter has to look very hard and go through many trials before he finds his wife again. Where in your life have you had to search long and hard before coming back to yourself?

7. The wounds sustained while caring for her children are ultimately what make the swan maiden unique from her sister swans and tether her to her life on the ground. In what ways has your mothering experience marked you and rendered you recognizable as an individual?

CHAPTER 2

Losing Control

Nothing exerts a stronger psychic effect upon . . .
children, than the life which the parents have not lived.

C. G. JUNG
COLLECTED WORKS, VOL. 15

Mothering is like a Tibetan sand mandala. We work long and lovingly to raise our child, knowing all the while that we will soon willingly say goodbye. We labor to adapt to each new stage, knowing that it will quickly pass. As soon as we get comfortable with parenting an infant, we find ourselves with a toddler and all of our certainty is overthrown. Just when we think we've grown used to parenting a teen, they're gone, and we now must learn how to mother a young adult. Again and again, we will have to come to terms with profound change and the concomitant loss of control.

Monica was a professional woman in her late forties with a fifteen-year-old daughter. She came to see me initially because her back pain was becoming crippling. Unwilling to consider surgery until she had exhausted every option, she had come to me to explore her emotional life to discover if there might be a link with her physical symptoms. In our first session, Monica told me that her back pain had started about two years earlier, shortly after Lily turned thirteen.

Monica and her husband, Karl, had adopted their daughter from China. Right from the beginning, they knew that Lily was very special.

"When Karl and I went to China to pick her up, every other baby was crying and wailing. Not Lily. She was serene. When Karl picked her up for the first time, she just looked at him and smiled," Monica explained.

As she grew, Lily continued to surprise and delight her parents. It soon became clear that she was quite gifted. She taught herself to read when she was three, and she made rapid progress at the piano the same year. Lily was also highly sensitive. Loud noises caused her great distress, and tense scenes in books or movies would send her into a tearful panic. As Monica and I discussed these memories of Lily's early years, I could sense her pride and delight but also her fear and defensiveness about her daughter.

"Other people didn't understand how hard it was to have a child like that," she told me.

When Lily was in kindergarten, she frequently became overwhelmed by the noise in the classroom and would come home tired and tearful. Monica and Karl approached the school and asked them to make changes aimed at alleviating some of Lily's tension during the day. When the school wouldn't comply with their request, Monica quit her job, pulled Lily out of school, and started homeschooling her.

"I loved homeschooling Lily!" Monica declared with emotion when I asked what this transition had been like for her. "We went to the library all the time. She was always reading. I loved reading when I was a girl too."

Lily continued to excel at music and academics throughout her grade-school years, competing in local and regional piano competitions, where she often took first place. Monica found enormous gratification pouring herself into Lily's development and studies. When asked about whether she missed her job working as director of education at a local art museum, Monica didn't hesitate. "There was nothing more compelling for me than Lily," she said.

Lily also continued to be an anxious child who had strong reactions to new situations. Monica had no doubt that protecting Lily from challenging circumstances was the right thing to do. When Lily, terrified of the water, cried at her first swim lesson, Monica pulled her out of the pool. "You're making a mistake!" the swim instructor called after her. "You've got to let her know she can survive her fear!" Monica was indignant. Even ten years on, as she told me this story, her face reddened with anger.

"Lily was beside herself. Just hysterical. And that woman wanted me to leave her there in the pool!" Lily didn't learn to swim until many years later.

When Lily was twelve, Michelle's family moved in down the street.

"At first, I was excited for Lily to have a friend in the neighborhood," Monica said. "It can be lonely being homeschooled." Soon, however, Lily was spending every afternoon and weekend at Michelle's house, and Monica noticed concerning behavior.

"Michelle was older than Lily by almost a year," Monica explained. "And she went to the public middle school in town, which is known for having a lot of kids with behavior problems."

Lily began imitating Michelle's edgy fashion, buying her clothes at thrift stores, and refusing to wear the feminine outfits Monica had always loved. Michelle got her nose pierced, and Lily became morose when Monica and Karl let her know that under no circumstances would she ever be allowed to get her nose pierced. Lily's behavior started to change in other ways as well. She no longer practiced piano and told her parents she wanted to quit. She lost interest in reading and academics and started spending all her time on the computer instead.

"We were very concerned about the influence that Michelle was having on Lily," Monica told me. "But the worst of it is that I feel like I've lost her. She and I were always so close. Around that time, she started acting so disdainful—like she hated me."

SEEKING SAFETY

Monica could not bear for Lily to experience pain or discomfort. As I got to know Monica better, I could hear the anxiety behind her words. I wasn't surprised to learn that Monica had suffered greatly growing up. Her home life had been chaotic. Her father was a heavy drinker, and her mother was overburdened with six children. As the eldest, Monica felt responsible for protecting her siblings from her father's drunken rages.

Monica had managed the chaos and anxiety of her childhood by exercising control over every aspect of her life where she could. She became an excellent student, winning prizes and awards at school. This strategy of keeping the chaos and fear at bay through overachievement and compulsive work had served her well throughout her adult life—until she became a mother. With a baby, it was difficult to control everything. Monica found herself anxious about all aspects of Lily's development. When Monica quit her job and no longer had the professional sphere in which to strive and achieve, being the perfect parent who kept Lily safe and happy took on even more importance.

As Lily entered adolescence, it was, of course, impossible for Monica to protect her from all harm, danger, and negative influence. This awakened in Monica the unresolved, terrifying feelings from her childhood of being imperiled and out of control. These were feelings and experiences she had managed but never faced and integrated. Lily's adolescent descent into teenage angst and experimentation brought these unresolved experiences back in full, terrifying force.

In truth, Monica's strategy for managing anxiety was just barely adequate. She performed well at work, and she had a solid marriage. But because her strategy involved avoiding all risk and vulnerability, it was, in fact, deadening. There was a lot of life that Monica was not living in an effort to keep herself together. She was known for cutting off relationships with friends whenever she felt threatened or challenged. She used the strictures of her religion to determine which ideas and experiences were okay and which weren't. Her anxiety limited her life in direct ways as well. She was a phobic driver and only went to a few proscribed places. Although she lived within thirty minutes of the arts and culture of downtown, she never went there. The toll this strategy took on her showed up in her body in the form of back pain—the thing that had caused her to seek treatment with me.

Therefore, although Monica appeared to be functioning adequately in her life, in fact, psychic growth had long ago come to a standstill. Just as her avoidance strategy had stifled her own life, her anxiety and need for control were also petrifying Lily's growth at a time when Lily needed to be moving toward independence.

This is a psychic situation that turns up frequently in fairy tales and myths. When Demeter lost her adolescent daughter to an abduction into the underworld by Hades, she wandered far and wide, distraught. At last, exhausted and grief-stricken, she sat beside a well in the town of Eleusis in the guise of an ordinary old woman. Some local young women approached her and offered her a job as a nursemaid for their beloved infant brother.

DEMETER AND PERSEPHONE

Like many a woman whose child has left her, Demeter assuaged her grief by caring for a baby. And like Monica, Demeter dealt with the grief of her first loss by trying to exercise control over the fate of the child in her care. The myth goes on to tell us that she fed the child ambrosia by day, and by night, she banked him in the fire as if he were a burning log. If Demeter had been allowed to continue these practices, the child would have become immortal like the gods. Unfortunately, the child's mother interrupted her one night. Seeing her son amid the smoldering fire, she shrieked.

At this point, Demeter revealed herself in all her goddess glory and rebuked the mother for her ignorance. She explained that the mother had made a terrible mistake, as the process of making the child "immortal and ageless" could not now be completed. Demeter then left the palace and went and sat alone in a temple that had been built for her. Here, she caused eternal winter to visit the land, not allowing seeds to grow so that people began to starve, and no offerings could be made to the gods. When Zeus saw what was going on, he sent messengers down to earth to beg Demeter to desist. She refused all attempts at reconciliation, saying that she would never restore the harvest until she saw her daughter. Zeus, at last, had to relent. A messenger was sent to Hades to retrieve Persephone, and Demeter was overjoyed to have her daughter restored to her, although for part of every year Persephone was required to return to Hades, where she ruled henceforward as Queen of the Dead.

Having lost her child, Demeter wanted to fix it so that the mortal boy in her care would become "immortal and ageless." I imagine that there is a part of every mother who would wish the same thing for her child. The immortal part would take care of our fears for our children's safety. Just imagine all the things we wouldn't have to worry about! And if our children were ageless, we would never worry about them growing older, growing up into ordinary adults destined to change, to leave us, and to suffer.

When my daughter was an infant, we lived next door to a delightful elderly woman. Mary had recently lost her husband to pancreatic cancer, and when he came up in conversation, tears sprang readily to her eyes. She and her husband had never had children, but a niece looked in on her every few weeks. Though Mary was one of those sunny people who always makes the best out of every situation, her loneliness was palpable. Her physical and emotional vulnerability as she faced the last few years of her life grieving and alone was evident and touched me to the quick. I held my beloved baby daughter and felt a deep wave of grief to think that one day, years from now, she might be bereft and alone in the world, and I would be gone, no longer able to comfort her. A part of me longed for a magical promise that she might always be well and happy.

It is fitting that it is only after her experience with the little boy that Demeter sinks into a grief so great that the crops fail. It is as if she has been able to avoid suffering by throwing herself into the project to keep the little boy perfect, unharmed, and unchanged. Of course, that project was bound to fail. None of us can protect our children from their fate, nor ultimately should we wish to. The entrance of the mother, which disturbed Demeter the night the little boy was in the fire, may seem like a mistake or a tragedy, but it is only as things should be. The mother was ensuring that her little boy would grow up and have a normal life, with all of the joys, heartaches, and disappointments that are our lot as part of being human.

So too, Monica had been deeply committed to the project of keeping Lily safe and untouched by the world. "I want her to stay as perfect as that day we first picked her up in the orphanage," she told me. Just like Demeter, Monica couldn't fully feel the grief and loss about Lily's growing up and about her own betrayed innocence until she had been forced to give up on the immortality project.

One of the great privileges of doing the work I do is being allowed to hear the wisdom individuals have culled throughout their life experience. One woman I worked with who had three grown sons shared with me a startling thought. Her sons had done some pretty risky and dangerous things in their young adulthood, such as motorcycling across the country or enlisting in the military and serving in combat. *How had she borne the fear?* I wondered. She answered the question without my having to ask it: "I knew these were dangerous things. At some point, I came to terms with the fact that they might die. But I knew that, if they did, they would have died doing something that really mattered to them." Her sons were committed to life. They wanted the fullest, best lives they could imagine for themselves. Living fully always entails risks of some kind. This mother, who was my patient, wanted her children to have full lives more than she wanted some illusory guarantee of their safety.

HINDERING GROWTH

In her memoir of motherhood, *The Middle of Everything*, writer Michelle Herman explores both her own mother's absence and her intense efforts to provide for her daughter what she did not get. Herman's mother had been depressed and emotionally unavailable. When her daughter was born, Herman had a clear parenting philosophy: *meet every need.* Herman writes, "The formula expands to what I come to think of as the commandments, fewer than ten, of motherly perfection. *Be available. Be attentive. Watch and listen. Keep your child from hunger, want, grief, loneliness, frustration.* Who could argue with this?"[1]

Like Demeter and Monica, Herman sought to protect her child from all pain and discomfort. But our inability to tolerate our children's discomfort teaches them that discomfort is intolerable. This imprisons them in fear and constricts their development. The author's daughter Grace began to suffer early on from anxiety, which culminated in debilitating obsessive-compulsive symptoms when she was six years old.

When we let our anxiety about a situation hold sway, we teach our children that it is not safe for them to leave us. We give in to that part of us that, like Demeter, wishes that nothing would change, that our children would never grow up and embrace their fate. Our fear can entrap our children, shutting them in with us in a frightening, tiny world. "I won't exist if you are not here," nine-year-old Grace tells her mother in terror as her mother is dropping her off at summer camp.[2]

With help from a therapist, Herman encouraged her daughter to separate from her—to sleep without her, go to friends' houses without her, go to birthday parties without her. Grace recovered, and Herman was able to see how she had contributed to Grace's difficulties separating. "I was stalling her—because I was stalled myself."[3] Herman states that, for her, pregnancy had conquered the loneliness she had known her whole life: "When I took that child in my arms for the first time, I experienced, beyond the absence of loneliness, the perfect connection to another human being. And I damn well wasn't going to give that up."[4]

Just as Michelle Herman could not continue on her path of growth and individuation while she was so invested in clinging to the ever-receding past of her daughter's infancy, neither could Monica grow and develop. Hanging tight to her daughter prevented her from facing her grief over her traumatic childhood. When we cling too tightly to our children, we hinder our growth as well as theirs. Our fear for the future, our grasping at the present even as it quickly fades into the past, keeps us stuck. As long as we fight against loss of all kinds, we squander our life, desperately trying to hold on to what we must be willing to let slip through our fingers. The kind of ossification seen in the experiences of both Herman and Monica is described in beautiful metaphoric language in the fairy tale "Little Brier Rose."

LITTLE BRIER ROSE

There once was a king and queen who were very sad because they had not been able to have children. At last, however, the queen gave birth to a baby girl, and a grand celebration was planned. The king and queen invited all of the fairies in the land, but because there were thirteen fairies and only twelve gold plates, they left one fairy out.

As the celebration ended, each fairy stood up and gave a gift to the princess. Virtue, beauty, equanimity, and all other manner of wonderful things were bequeathed. The eleventh fairy had just imparted her offering when the thirteenth fairy walked in. Angry that she had been overlooked, she cried out, "Because you did not invite me, your daughter will prick herself with a spindle when she is fifteen and fall dead."

Amid the shocked and horrified silence, the twelfth fairy stood up. "I cannot undo the curse," she said. "But I can soften it. Your daughter will not die, but she will fall into a hundred-year sleep." The king, hoping to protect his beloved child, ordered that every spindle in the kingdom be destroyed.

The princess grew to be a great beauty and was beloved by all who knew her. One day, when she had just turned fifteen, the king and the queen had gone away, leaving her alone in the castle. She walked from room to room, going wherever she wished. Finally, she came upon an old tower. She climbed the stairs until she came to a small door, which sprang open easily at her touch. Inside sat an old woman spinning flax. She was curiously drawn to the old woman and watched her spinning with fascination. At length she said that she would like to try her hand at spinning. No sooner had she picked up the spindle than she pricked herself with it and fell into a deep sleep.

The sleep spread throughout the entire castle. The king and queen had just returned home, and they and all of their attendants lay down in the hall and slept. The cook and other servants slept. The dogs in the kennel, the horses in the stable, the pigeons on the roof, and the flies on the wall all slept. Even the fire in the hearth flickered out, and the wind itself stopped blowing.

As the castle and its inhabitants slept on, a thick thorn hedge grew up around the castle. Year after year it grew until it completely surrounded the castle and hid it from view. A legend grew up about the beautiful Little Brier Rose asleep in the castle, waiting to be rescued. As the years passed, young men would try to fight their way through the thick hedge, but they all became stuck through with thorns and died miserably.

At last, the hundred years had passed. A prince traveling through heard the legend of Little Brier Rose from an old man. He determined that he would try to penetrate the thorn hedge and see Little Brier Rose for himself. No matter how the old man tried to dissuade him, he could not be convinced to give up the quest. He came to the hedge, and in place of thorns, there were beautiful fragrant blossoms. The hedge parted, allowing him to enter easily, though it closed again behind him.

Arriving at the castle, he was amazed at the slumbering dogs, people, pigeons, and horses. All was absolutely quiet and still save for the soft breathing of the sleepers. The prince threaded his way through the castle, stepping over sleeping inhabitants. At long last, he found his way into the tower where a century ago, Little Brier Rose had been so entranced by the old woman spinning. He saw her sleeping there on the bed onto which she had fallen, and he found her so beautiful he could not help himself. He leaned down and gave her a gentle kiss. At that moment, she awoke. She gazed up at him smiling.

Together they descended to find everyone in the castle gradually awakening. The spotted dogs stretched and yawned. The pigeons fluttered on the roof. The king and queen awoke, dusting themselves off. The fire sputtered back to life and continued cooking the roast. Little Brier Rose and her prince were married and lived in great happiness and splendor till the end of their days.

Like Little Brier Rose, Lily was the precious child who was longed for and despaired of before she finally arrived. In psychological terms, Little Brier Rose's birth is the granting of our heart's desire after a long, tearful duration of fretful waiting. For many women, becoming a mother will feel like this, regardless of the precise circumstances of how this comes to pass. When a woman has struggled to become a mother because of infertility or other reasons, the much-longed-for birth can truly feel miraculous.

Amid the great joy that a new mother feels as she gazes at her infant, she takes in his perfection. He is all potential, as yet utterly pure and undiminished. Understandably, we as mothers may wish to protect that purity and possibility by shielding him always from harm. We can see this in Demeter's desire to render her charge invulnerable and unchanging. We see it in the king's decree to rid his kingdom of spindles. Michelle Herman gives voice to this wish when she vows that she will meet every need for her baby daughter. And we see it in the attitudes and actions of Karl and Monica, who wished to insulate Lily from any struggle or discomfort.

THE THIRTEENTH FAIRY

The thirteenth fairy represents an uncomfortable reality that doesn't quite fit with our ideas of what we would like for our lives. We, therefore, wish to avoid or ignore her. Thirteen is a number associated with darkness, transgression, and evil. The thirteenth fairy symbolizes the parts of ourselves we would rather not know—aggression, envy, demandingness. The thirteenth fairy is alive in us, and she will undoubtedly wish to be included in our lives as we mother. If we don't set a place at our table for our dark qualities, they are likely to paradoxically bring about the very wounding of our children that we aim to avoid. Monica and Karl were so determined to make Lily's life enchanted in every way that she grew up to be delicate, thin-skinned, and susceptible to being easily seduced.

Like the king and queen of the tale, Monica wished to safeguard Lily from life's initiatory wounding. Getting rid of all the spindles is a refusal to mourn, to accept that life always flows forward into the future and things that we love will change and be lost. Adolescence is a time when, for many, there is a kind of dark passage, a departure from the safety of childhood that sometimes is quite perilous and almost always looks so to the parental eye. But when we as mothers try too hard to hedge our child against life's ordinary affronts, we risk allowing our growth to stagnate as well as that of our child. The ultimate psychological goal of life is to continue to become increasingly conscious. When we get wrapped up in protecting our children, we forego the opportunity to grow and bring more of ourselves into consciousness. When we insulate ourselves and our children from challenge and loss, we cease to grow. The tale is very clear on this point—the life of the entire family comes to a complete standstill when Little Brier Rose falls asleep.

What are we to make of the symbols of spinning and spindle? I remember being perplexed at this detail of the story even as a child. According to my admittedly only theoretical knowledge of spindles, they are not particularly sharp, so it seems like an odd object on which to prick one's finger. Freudian interpretations of this tale suggest that the spindle is a phallus, and her encounter with the old woman in the tower is, therefore, a first sexual experience. To my mind, the symbolism goes much deeper than that. Spinning and spindles are associated symbolically with the goddess. In many cultures, there are goddesses who are the spinners and weavers of fate. As we saw when we looked at "The Two Caskets," in Greek mythology, the Fates are a group of three goddesses who control destiny. One of these is Clotho, the spinner, who is often pictured with a distaff and spindle. Little Brier Rose's visit to the tower, therefore, is nothing less than an encounter with her fate. As mothers, we must be prepared for the day when our children will find their own fate, even if this frightens us.

Having been so sheltered and treated as "special" her whole life, Little Brier Rose has no sense of agency or self-efficacy with which to meet her fate. She is, of course, drawn to the spinning woman who holds this great and powerful secret of destiny. In response to being pricked, Little Brier Rose falls passively asleep. It will take a long time before her thick, prickly defenses can be penetrated. In the Grimm's version of the tale, the prince happens to kiss her as she awakens. He does not awaken her. These two events happen at the same time for an important reason. The prince is an image of the heroine's "princely" qualities—adventurousness, courage, fortitude. These were conspicuously absent while she was in the sleep of unconsciousness. Only after the passage of sufficient time can she awaken to these qualities in herself. So it is often the case for young women who may not have been allowed to develop their sense of agency and fierceness adequately. They may remain unconscious for many years, sleepwalking passively through their lives. For most of us who live in such a way, something prince-like usually does wake up in us at some point, helping us to move out into life more actively.

We can try to prepare our children for their fate, but we cannot protect them from it. Attempting to do so will have a deadening effect. Monica came to some awareness of how she had allowed her own life to become constricted as a result of her well-intentioned fear and concern for Lily. Poignantly, she shared with me that she had realized she no longer had any dreams for herself.

"I've been a jogger since I was fifteen," she told me. "My whole life, once I put my headphones and running shoes on, I was in my own little world. I would always have the most wonderful daydreams while I was jogging. When I was in my teens, I daydreamed about moving out of my crazy house. Later, I would imagine fun things, like really knocking it out of the park at a work presentation. I imagined Karl before I ever met him. I even daydreamed Lily when we were waiting so long to have a child!" Monica's eyes were filling with tears as she spoke. "I went running the other day," she said, her voice breaking. "And I realized that for many years now, I have been only daydreaming about Lily. I've imagined her performing downtown when she is older. I've seen myself accompanying her to piano competitions across the country. But I can't dream about those things anymore. And then I told myself I would daydream about me, about *my* life during that run. And I couldn't. I didn't have any dreams left for myself."

Like Demeter, Monica had some grieving to do before fertile possibility could awaken again for her. She had to grieve the fantasied future she had imagined for Lily and accept the daughter she had. She had to grieve for the end of her youth as she faced the second half of her life. The hardest work of all was to grieve her innocence, which had been violated at an early age because of the trauma she endured.

HOLDING ON

We may forestall psychic growth for ourselves and our children by shielding them from pain, discomfort, or challenge. We can also hold on too tightly for too long.

Karen was a divorced professional in her fifties. When she started working with me, she had recently learned that her twenty-nine-year-old daughter had once again relapsed and was actively drinking. Though Karen had been dealing with her daughter's alcoholism for years, this relapse hit her particularly hard.

"Elizabeth and I have been doing this dance for so long," she told me at our first appointment. "She falls down, and I have always been there to pick her up. It's dysfunctional, but it has worked, and we have both known our place. But this time, I just can't do it again."

Elizabeth had lost her license as a result of driving while intoxicated. Unable to get to work reliably, she was in danger of losing her job. As she always had before, she turned to her mother, asking if she could move in with her temporarily to make for an easier commute. Karen was torn. On the one hand, if she didn't let Elizabeth move back in, there was a good chance that Elizabeth would lose her job—one that had taken Elizabeth a long time to find. On the other hand, Karen was beginning to see how much of her own life she had not lived as a result of the years she had spent worrying about Elizabeth.

As is often the case in families in which there is an addiction, Karen found herself in an unhealthy helping pattern with Elizabeth. On the surface, she resented Elizabeth's excessive need for her help. But on a deeper level, she had organized much of her life and sense of self around her role as Elizabeth's support system. A deeply empathic and principled person, she wanted to do the right thing for her struggling daughter. As we sat together turning over the decision as to whether to let Elizabeth move in, I noticed that Karen spoke only about her daughter's needs.

"Karen," I asked her one day, "what do *you* want to have happen in this situation? What would be best for you?" She shifted in her seat before replying. "Well, I don't want Elizabeth to lose her job. That would be such a blow. I worry it will take even longer for her to get back on her feet. There isn't much of a place for her to stay in this house, but I think I can put a futon in the living room since it is only for a few months."

When I pointed out to her that I had asked her what *she* wanted but that her reply was only about her *daughter*, Karen was silent for a long moment before responding. "I don't think I even know what I want," she said.

As Karen and I probed her feelings around this decision, she began to realize that part of her would feel lost if Elizabeth got better and moved on. Being there for Elizabeth provided a clear structure and meaning for Karen's life. It distracted her from the important and sobering questions she had about what she wanted to do with her remaining decades. It helped her avoid the anxiety of considering whether or not to try dating. There were many decisions she did not have to face. In many ways, it made her life, paradoxically, simple.

"Being a mother was the most compelling thing I have ever done," Karen told me. "You feel needed. What you do feels important. You know you really matter to at least this one person."

Part of Karen's decision about how to support Elizabeth's recovery involved her coming to terms with her changing role. She needed to mourn the time of her life when she had been raising Elizabeth—a part of her life she had loved a great deal and now missed. There were many tears as we recalled those years together. She admitted that looking into the years ahead sometimes filled her with dread at their emptiness. She could see how, in part, she was clinging to Elizabeth's continued need for her to provide meaning.

However, like Monica, Karen's life had stalled. The focus of all of her very considerable energy had gone into Elizabeth for many, many years. She had long thought about leaving her job and starting her own business, but she was afraid to do so. She admitted that Elizabeth had provided a comfortable excuse to avoid taking this step. She had longed her whole adult life to go back to Spain, where she had lived briefly as a child, and to spend several months there becoming fluent in Spanish. Elizabeth's addiction had allowed her to put off this goal as well.

The Japanese fairy tale "Princess Moonbeam" is another story that makes it clear that in order for us to continue to grow, we need to let our children go when the time comes.

PRINCESS MOONBEAM

A woodcutter and his wife lived together near a forest. They were very unhappy because they had no children. The mother prayed that a child might be sent to her. The next evening, the couple witnessed a gentle light as it fell to earth and landed among the bamboo. Going in search of the light, the woodcutter found a beautiful little being gently glowing with a strange light, resting amid the bamboo. "Who are you?" he said to the little creature, who was no bigger than a doll.

"I am Princess Moonbeam. My mother is the Moon Lady, and she has sent me here to be your child so that I may do a good deed." The woodcutter brought the delicate little creature home to his wife, who laughed with joy. She carefully dressed and bathed the little princess and began to care for her as lovingly as if she were her own child.

Princess Moonbeam sometimes felt homesick for her moon mother and her home among the stars. Though she loved her earth parents, she looked forward to the not-too-distant day when she would be able to go home.

As she grew, Princess Moonbeam became even lovelier year by year. Her parents adored her, and all who met her were charmed. In time, reports of her beauty spread far and wide, and the emperor himself came to Princess Moonbeam's humble home to gaze upon her with his own eyes. Her parents were overjoyed to receive such an esteemed guest. When Moonbeam came out bearing fresh cakes and tea for the emperor, he merely stared at her in silence for a moment. "This is the most beautiful woman I have ever seen!" he said at last. "This woman will be my wife!" Princess Moonbeam remained calm.

"I am afraid that is impossible," she said. Her parents were horrified. "Oh, Daughter! You cannot speak to the emperor this way!"

The emperor bellowed in anger. "Who are you to defy me? I am the emperor! I get whatever I want! I demand you come with me to my palace tonight!"

"I cannot come with you," explained Moonbeam. "My time here is coming to an end. See? My moon mother comes to fetch me even now!" And as Moonbeam pointed to the sky, her parents and the emperor saw a descending beam of silvery light, aglow with shimmering star spirits.

"Guards!" shouted the emperor. "Surround this house! Shoot the intruders!" His men raised their bows and loosed their arrows, but as they did so, they all turned to stone, along with the emperor. As the arrows rained back to down earth, a beautiful jade-green woman descended from the starry staircase. "Moon Mother!" shouted Princess Moonbeam joyfully. The two ran to each other and embraced.

Moonbeam's earthly parents saw all of this from where they stood. They began to cry, knowing that their daughter would be leaving them.

Princess Moonbeam ran back to find them, hugging and kissing them warmly. "Thank you for all you have done for me!" she said. "I will never forget you!" Then Princess Moonbeam ascended the beam of light with her moon mother, waving goodbye to her earthly parents. As a parting gift, she turned their tears to fireflies, so that on summer nights, they would always be able to remember her.

As in "Little Brier Rose," this fairy tale concerns itself with a child miraculously delivered after long years of hopeful waiting. Brier Rose and Moonbeam are both the treasured child, much beloved, and carefully protected. That Moonbeam is merely "loaned" to the childless couple underscores a poignant truth about parenting. We may gestate our children in our womb, knitting up their form and nourishing them with our blood, but they never really belong to us. In the first months after birth, we may be able to bask in an illusory oceanic unity with our child, but this lovely fantasy gets shattered with toddlerhood, if not before. Toddlers remind us several times per day that they are separate from us, famously asserting their budding individuality by the incessant use of "No!" In more painful ways, our teenagers will also frequently remind us of how fundamentally distinct they are from us as they reject our values and even our affection.

The emperor in "Princess Moonbeam" symbolizes a drive to power and control that can be understood as an aspect of the parent-child relationship. When we as mothers feel overly invested in our children, we may wish to exert control over them to keep them from leaving us. When we persist in trying to exercise control, our lives become static and sterile—we turn to stone.

DESCENDING INTO MOURNING

During the early years of my children's education, we homeschooled. Those years were full of libraries, museums, and road trips. We grew crystals, raised butterflies, and mummified chickens (which are still buried somewhere in the backyard). I treasured the time spent with my children in this way, but not a week went by when I didn't ask myself whether their educational interests were being best served. And each week for years, the answer that came back was yes. Until it didn't. One day when my son was nine, a friend casually mentioned that there were spots open at a local private school, and somehow I just *knew* at that moment that it was time for my son to go. I felt *sad*, and that told me that it was indeed time for something to end.

At home later, I told him I was wondering if he might enjoy going to school. "You know, Mom," he told me. "I am really glad you said that because I have been wondering the same thing."

I felt such grief! Over the course of the next week I cried many times, although I was careful to do so in private. Throughout the time that we were applying to schools, I would occasionally revisit this decision. My son was bright, creative, and mildly dyslexic. How would any school be able to do right by him? I still felt an impulse to hold him close and protect him. There were days when I wished he would change his mind. One surprisingly warm rainy Thursday in November, I invited him to go for a walk with me. We splashed through puddles as we had done when he was a tiny boy, and my heart hurt to think we would have fewer chances to spend time together in this way.

It was tempting to convince myself that he needed to stay at home with me so that things could remain as they had been. In truth, it was right for both of us to move on from our homeschooling phase. When he started school the following year, he loved it and did well. And I entered a new stage of my career where I had more time to devote to my clinical work and my writing. When we relinquish our need to exert control over our lives and that of our children, we may drop into grief, but this is a necessary descent into mourning for what has been lost. Only by allowing ourselves to feel our sadness can we reawaken to the new possibilities and pleasures offered by the next stage of our lives.

For understandable reasons, it was difficult for Karen to give up control. Karen fought against releasing Elizabeth to her fate. Her task was not an easy one. She needed to offer an appropriate amount of continued support to Elizabeth while still setting a boundary that required Elizabeth to find her way so that Karen could live her life. For Karen, this meant helping Elizabeth identify a reliable way to get to work without allowing her to move back in. This was a tremendously difficult thing for Karen to do. She was surprised and overwhelmed by the amount of grief she felt as she cut this cord of dependency that had kept them connected for so long. One day during this intense grieving process, Karen brought the poem "On Children" by Kahlil Gibran to her session with me.

> Your children are not your children.
> They are the sons and daughters of Life's longing for itself.
> They come through you but not from you,
> And though they are with you yet they belong not to you.
> You may give them your love but not your thoughts,
> For they have their own thoughts.
> You may house their bodies but not their souls,
> For their souls dwell in the house of tomorrow,
> which you cannot visit, not even in your dreams.
> You may strive to be like them,
> but seek not to make them like you.
> For life goes not backward nor tarries with yesterday.
> You are the bows from which your children
> as living arrows are sent forth.
> The archer sees the mark upon the path of the infinite,
> and He bends you with His might
> that His arrows may go swift and far.
> Let your bending in the archer's hand be for gladness;
> For even as He loves the arrow that flies
> so He loves also the bow that is stable.[5]

Karen and I both teared up as she read this poem aloud in our session.

"I want to be a stable bow," she told me tearfully. "I want to let Elizabeth fly."

Karen had to let Elizabeth live her own life, even if that meant watching as Elizabeth made very different choices—and even mistakes. Releasing Elizabeth was painful, but doing so gave Karen the opportunity to turn her attention back to her journey and also hopefully allowed Elizabeth to fly.

BLACK SWANS AND CONTROLLING QUEENS

The 2010 film *Black Swan* paints a dark picture of what can happen when we give in to the drive for control imaged by the emperor in "Princess Moonbeam." The film follows Nina (played by Natalie Portman), a dancer in the New York City Ballet. Though Nina is an adult, she lives with her mother, Erica (Barbara Hershey). The film makes it clear throughout that mother and daughter are pathologically enmeshed and that growth for both of them has been stultified.

At the beginning of the movie, we see Nina's bedroom. It is pink and frilly, filled with stuffed animals and other items that indicate the room has not been redecorated since she was a young teen. Her jewelry is kept in a little girl's jewelry box, the kind where a plastic ballerina spins to tinny music when it is opened. We watch as Erica serves Nina breakfast and packs her daughter's shoulder bag with snacks and extra clothing. Erica's behavior toward Nina infantilizes her daughter. This dynamic is stressed further throughout the film as Erica helps her daughter undress, removes her earrings, and clips her fingernails. Erica's controlling behavior extends to the physical space the two women inhabit. Neither the bathroom door nor Nina's bedroom door has a lock on it. The film makes much of this, with Nina desperately trying to shut her mother out by jamming her door closed with a piece of wood.

Becoming a fully sexual being is a key way we separate from our parents. We see that Erica takes care to thwart Nina's sexual exploration. At one point, Nina lies in her bed and begins to masturbate when she is interrupted by a rustle and a snore. She peeks from under the covers to find her mother asleep in the chair next to her bed. When Nina comes home from an uncharacteristic night out at a bar and drunkenly boasts of fucking two guys, her mother becomes enraged and tries to silence her by forcing her hand over Nina's mouth. "You're not my Nina now!" she shouts.[6]

The film makes it clear that Erica's growth and development as a person stopped some time ago. Her preoccupation with controlling her daughter's life has resulted in her giving up on having any life of her own. Erica appears to be infatuated with Nina as a child. The walls of Erica's bedroom are filled with paintings she has made of Nina as a young girl posing in a tutu. It is clear that Erica paints these pictures obsessively, always working on another one. When Nina begins to be courted by the company director, her mother expresses concern. Irritated, Nina (untruthfully) denies that he has "tried anything." Erica explains that she wouldn't want Nina to "make the same mistake she did" by getting pregnant and setting aside her career. "What career?" Nina asks snidely. "The one I gave up to have you," replies Erica.[7] Erica is a mother who can't let go, and Nina is a child who has never grown up. Nina's desperate attempts to separate from her mother don't go well. She is too psychologically fragile, and her efforts to differentiate herself from her mother lead her into self-destruction and mental illness.

Did you notice that we have returned at the end to a swan story? This isn't a coincidence. If we mother too much like the parents in "Little Brier Rose" or the emperor in "Princess Moonbeam," refusing to release our children when the time comes, we run the risk that our daughters will become selkie brides or swan maidens, girlish and undeveloped. Controlling queens and flighty swans are two sides of one coin, a pair of opposites. Both potentials exist in all of us. It may be your fate to be a swan or selkie at one point in your life, and a controlling queen at another time. Daughters become mothers who have daughters, and thus the cycle recapitulates itself. If you are a selkie, becoming a mother may be an opportunity to separate and grow up. If you are a controlling queen, your child's departure may be bitterly painful, but it will create an opportunity for you to journey deeper into your depths. When we consciously submit to what this cycle of development demands of us, we open ourselves up to heartbreak and loss. We also allow ourselves to become life's fertile field, nourishing whatever seeks to be born through us into the world.

Questions for Reflection
for Losing Control

1. So much about mothering means adapting to a loss of control. Where in your life have you lost control as a result of being a mother? How have you responded to this?

2. Both of the stories featured in this chapter begin with the parents' heartbreak and longing over not having children. What have you yearned for with all your heart? Did you receive it? What was that like?

3. The thirteenth fairy represents an inconvenient truth about ourselves, one we would prefer to exclude in the interest of proper presentation according to superficial conventions. The thirteenth fairy presumably would have been an ally if she had been invited to the party. Excluding her turns her into an enemy. What part of yourself would you prefer to exclude? (Perhaps it is your greed? Envy? Pettiness?)

4. When you have excluded this part, how have you been cursed because of it? (Maybe you were overwhelmed with anger? Maybe you were taken advantage of in some situation because you didn't adequately protect yourself?)

5. On her fifteenth birthday, the princess finds the old woman in the room and is strangely attracted to the spindle. Where in your life have you felt inexplicably drawn to something? Perhaps it was something that proved harmful or dangerous in the short term, but perhaps not? How might this have been an encounter with your fate?

6. In what situations has it been difficult for you to allow your child to encounter his or her own fate?

7. In "Princess Moonbeam," the bamboo cutter and his wife realize that they have been blessed by a precious gift that is ultimately not theirs to keep. The emperor tries to exercise worldly authority over Moonbeam, who belongs to a celestial realm where he has no sway. His efforts to control the princess are hubristic, and he is punished accordingly. When have you tried hard to control something that wasn't yours to control? What happened?

CHAPTER 3
Losing Ourselves

To be human means to be wounded. The
story of one's life grows around wounds that
open to what is truly, deeply human.

MICHAEL MEADE
THE WATER OF LIFE

Getting thrown down a metaphorical well is always profoundly disorienting, and it can certainly seem like the end of us. Confusion and despair are unavoidable parts of being human, and they will undoubtedly visit you during your experience of motherhood. There may be times when you feel a profound sense of disconnection from your children—and yourself. In early motherhood, this might mean being visited by the specter of postpartum depression or its lesser form, postpartum blues. But we will undoubtedly have the experience of losing ourselves at other times during our mothering journey, even if just fleetingly. For example, when your preteen daughter asserts her independence and it occurs to you that you don't actually like her, you may be pulled up short by the recognition that you have withdrawn some of your energy from the relationship. As your children enter high school and their independence looms, you might find yourself feeling more compelled by work and career than you have in years. It can be disorienting to realize that the nature of our relationship with our kids is shifting, in part because it calls our identity as mothers into question.

DISCONNECTION

My client Rachel is now a grandmother, but she entered treatment with me in part to try to come to terms with the remorse and sadness she felt over the loss of connection with her children. Rachel's story of being disconnected from herself and her children is a rather extreme example. You may not have lived a version of this story, but you might still be able to find yourself in it. Raised by a single mom in a rural area, Rachel grew up poor. Tall and stunningly beautiful, she hadn't finished high school when she was signed as a model. She moved to New York when she was seventeen and became swept up in a life that involved a lot of alcohol, drugs—and attention from older men. Within a year, Rachel was engaged to a man from a wealthy family. She became pregnant shortly after that. Rachel remembers that the arrival of her first child brought great tenderness, but also fear. She was just nineteen years old and felt totally out of her depth when it came to taking care of a baby. When her mother-in-law swooped in and insisted on hiring a team of around-the-clock nurses and nannies, Rachel didn't object. Freed from her duties as a mother, Rachel more or less continued her life as a Greenwich Village socialite immersed in the art and drug culture of the time. The birth of her second child brought only a brief disruption to this existence, as this second baby was quickly turned over to the nurse as well.

Rachel never had a chance to grow into her role as a mother. As the children grew, she continued to feel out of her element, the more so as her husband and mother-in-law had strong ideas about their upbringing. Because she felt so incompetent around her children, she often chose to spend time away from them, leading her to feel even more disconnected and incompetent. She has a memory of a summer in Greece when she was alone with her two young daughters for many weeks at a time. Removed from the heady swirl of her life in Manhattan and with minimal interference from her husband's family, Rachel spent her days playing with and caring for her children. Today, she inevitably tears up as she remembers the sweetness of this summer.

The connection she felt with her children that summer was not to be replicated, however. By the time her girls were in grade school,

Rachel's drinking and drug habit had become a noticeable problem. When Rachel was thirty-two, her husband left her, taking the girls with him. Rachel was granted only minimal contact with her children. By the time they were adults, they had estranged themselves completely.

Today, Rachel has been sober for almost twenty years. She is in touch with both of her children, although her older daughter communicates with her only a few times per year. Her younger daughter is in her life in a consistent way, however, and Rachel has enjoyed being able to be present as a grandmother in a way she never was as a mother. Part of Rachel's task in therapy has been to grieve for the lost opportunity to be a mother to her children.

GETTING AND STAYING ATTACHED

A friend of mine with three small children used to laughingly remind herself daily that parenting was supposed to be fun and enjoyable. She was pointing to an important truth. Neurobiologists have pointed out that our brains come equipped with a reward system that helps us to be open to one another and to new experiences and a stress system that locks us into a defensive, closed-off state. As Daniel A. Hughes and Jonathan Baylin write in their book *Brain-Based Parenting*, "Love is a state of openness to another person, and it competes in our brains and bodies with closed states of self-defense. Parenting well requires the ability to stay open and engaged with our children most of the time, not closed off to them as we defend ourselves against feeling unsafe or insecure."[1]

It is the natural order of things for mothers to attach to their children. When the mother-child relationship is proceeding as it ought, the mother feels gratified and fulfilled when she meets the needs of her child. The baby cries. The mother goes to her and picks her up—and the baby stops crying. This sends the mother a strong message about her competence. Caring for her child helps her feel capable and confident. Mothering, then, becomes a source of self-worth. In such a circumstance, parenting feels both deeply meaningful and intensely pleasurable—at least part of the time. It is nearly as important that we enjoy our children as that we love them, for pleasure in another is the very stuff of robust attachment.

When, for some reason, you don't feel competent in your role as a mother, you may find that your children are sources of anxiety, insecurity, or shame. You might then understandably find yourself avoiding them because you feel you won't be up to the task of caring for them. This can lead you to feel less attached, which may make it more difficult for you to care for them, causing you to feel more distressed and demoralized as a mother, creating a self-reinforcing cycle of disconnection. And because you will likely feel intense shame and inadequacy, you not only feel as though you have lost a sense of connection to your children. You also feel as though you have lost—or perhaps never found—an authentic connection to yourself.

Every parent will, at some point, experience such a pattern of disconnection at least momentarily. When we are worried about a difficult issue at work and find ourselves lashing out angrily at our toddler when he is noisy; when we are irritable and preoccupied while helping with homework; when we see our teen making poor decisions and become so frightened for her that we find ourselves wanting to avoid her—these are examples of temporary experiences of what Hughes and Baylin call "blocked parental care." Many mothers experience such minor disconnections as distressing, but they are an entirely normal part of parenting and occur even daily for most of us. The ordinary waxing and waning of openness to our children throughout the day is likely necessary and healthy. In essence, it allows a child space to develop a sense of self as someone separate from us.

However, when such patterns of disconnection become chronic, we may find ourselves stepping back from our role as a mother. This is what happened to Rachel. Such significant ruptures in connection can occur at any point and for many different reasons. A prominent feature of postpartum depression is that the maternal reward system that makes us want to move toward our children doesn't function properly. A mother with postpartum depression may have fantasies of leaving the baby or at least feels no pleasure in being with him. This is usually accompanied by feelings of incompetence and low self-worth.

The stresses associated with poverty can also trigger a longer-term breakdown in the parental care system. When a mother is depleted, overwhelmed, and without adequate support, she may get locked into the defensive, closed-off state much of the time. Such chronic states of fear and defensiveness cut us off from our children—and our sense of aliveness. It can feel as though we have lost ourselves.

Adolescence is another period when significant disconnections can occur. If a sense of competence as a parent is key to our enjoying and connecting with our kids, it's easy to understand why the teenage years present such a challenge in this regard. While toddlers can be maddeningly irritating, they are also commonly adorable, cuddly, and hilarious. Teens, on the other hand, can sometimes be mostly difficult, frustrating—and even frightening. For some of us, the rewards of parenting a teen can be few and far between. If you are parenting a difficult teen and you are not getting the positive experiences of connection and competence, you may find yourself wanting to disconnect. It's helpful to remember that such an urge can be in service to your child's development. Adolescence is, after all, a time that they begin to separate from us. Even in the midst of our desire to shut down and withdraw, we need to find a way to trust ourselves and know that we have much to offer even when our teen is not reflecting this back to us.

A Grimm's fairy tale offers us an image of blocked parental care as a result of profound emotional wounding. It concerns a mother who has become deeply depressed and, therefore, cannot protect or stay connected to her children—or herself.

THE SIX SWANS

A king was once hunting in a great forest, and he chased his prey so eagerly that none of his men could follow him. As evening approached, he stopped and looked around, and saw that he was lost. He looked for a way out of the woods, but he could not find one. Then he saw an old woman approaching him. He did not know that she was a witch.

"My dear woman," he said to her, "can you show me the way through the woods?"

"Oh, yes, Your Majesty," she answered, "I can indeed. However, there is one condition, and if you do not fulfill it, you will never get out of these woods, and you will die here of hunger."

"What sort of condition is it?" asked the king.

"I have a beautiful daughter," said the old woman. "If you will make her your queen, I will show you the way out of the woods."

The king was so frightened that he consented, and the old woman led him to her cottage, where her daughter was sitting by the fire. She received the king as if she had been expecting him. He saw that she was very beautiful, but despite this, he did not like her, and he could not look at her without secretly shuddering.

After he had lifted the girl onto his horse, the old woman showed him the way, and the king arrived again at his royal castle, where the wedding was celebrated.

The king had been married before, and by his first wife he had seven children—six boys and one girl. He loved them more than anything else in the world.

Fearing that the stepmother might not treat them well, he took them to a secluded castle that stood in the middle of a forest. It was so well hidden, and the way was so difficult to find, that he would not have found it if a wise woman had not given him a ball of magic yarn. Whenever he threw it down in front of him, it would unwind itself and show him the way.

However, the king went out to his dear children so often that the queen took notice of his absence. She was curious and wanted to know what he was doing out there all alone in the woods. She bribed his servants, who told her the king's secret, and they gave her the ball of yarn.

She made some little shirts of white silk that had a magic charm sewn into them. Then one day, when the king had ridden out hunting, she took the little shirts and went into the woods. The ball of yarn showed her the way.

The children, seeing that someone was approaching from afar, thought that their dear father was coming to them. Full of joy, they ran to meet him. Then she threw one of the shirts over each of them, and when the shirts touched their bodies, they were transformed into swans, and they flew away over the woods.

The queen went home very pleased, believing that she had gotten rid of her stepchildren. However, the girl had not run out with her brothers, and the queen knew nothing about her.

The next day, the king went to visit his children, but he found no one there except the girl.

"Where are your brothers?" asked the king.

"Oh, dear Father," she answered, "they have gone away and left me alone."

Then she told him that from her window she had seen how her brothers had flown away over the woods as swans. She showed him the feathers that they had dropped into the courtyard and that she had gathered up.

The king mourned, but he did not think that the queen had done this wicked deed. Fearing that the girl would be stolen from him as well, he wanted to take her with him. But his daughter was afraid of her stepmother and begged the king to let her stay just this one more night in the castle in the woods.

The poor girl thought, *I can no longer stay here. I will go and look for my brothers.*

When night came, she ran away into the woods. She walked and walked until she found a hunter's hut. Inside, she found a room with six little beds. She crawled under one of the beds and went to sleep.

The sun was about to go down when she heard a rushing sound and saw six swans fly in through the window. Landing on the floor, they blew on one another and blew all their feathers off. Then their swanskins came off just like shirts. The girl looked at them and recognized her brothers. She was happy and crawled out from beneath the bed. The brothers were no less happy to see their little sister, but their happiness did not last long.

"You cannot stay here," they said to her. "This is a robbers' den. If they come home and find you, they will murder you."

"Can't you protect me?" asked the little sister.

"No," they answered. "We can take off our swan-skins for only a quarter-hour each evening. Only during that time do we have our human forms. After that, we are again transformed into swans."

Crying, the little sister said, "Can you not be redeemed?"

"Alas, no," they answered. "The conditions are too difficult. You would not be allowed to speak or to laugh for six years, and in that time, you would have to sew together six little shirts from asters for us. And if a single word were to come from your mouth, all your work would be lost."

After the brothers had said this, the quarter-hour was over, and they flew out the window again as swans.

Nevertheless, the girl firmly resolved to redeem her brothers. She left the hunter's hut, went to the middle of the woods, seated herself in a tree, and there spent the night. The next morning, she went out and gathered asters and began to sew. She could not speak with anyone, and she had no desire to laugh. She sat there, looking only at her work.

After she had already spent a long time there, it happened that the king of the land was hunting in these woods. His huntsmen came to the tree where the girl was sitting.

They called to her, saying, "Who are you?" But she did not answer.

"Come down to us," they said. "We will not harm you."

She only shook her head. When they pressed her further with questions, she threw her golden necklace down to them, thinking that this would satisfy them. But they did not stop, so she then threw her belt down to them, and when this did not help, her garters, and then—one thing at a time—everything that she had on and could do without until, finally, she had nothing left but her shift.

The huntsmen, however, not letting themselves be dissuaded, climbed the tree, lifted the girl down, and took her to the king.

The king asked, "Who are you? What are you doing in that tree?"

But she did not answer. He asked her in every language that he knew, but she remained as speechless as a fish. Because she was so beautiful, the king's heart was touched and he fell deeply in love with her. He put his cloak around her, lifted her onto his horse in front of himself, and took her to his castle. There he had her dressed in rich garments, but no one could get a word from her.

At the table, he seated her by his side, and her modest manners and courtesy pleased him so much that he said, "She will be my wife."

A few days later, they were married.

Now the king had a wicked mother who was dissatisfied with this marriage and spoke ill of the young queen. "Who knows," she said, "from whence the girl who cannot speak comes. She is not worthy of a king."

A year later, after the queen had brought her first child into the world, the wicked mother took it away from her while she was asleep and smeared the queen's mouth with blood. Then she went to the king and accused her of being a cannibal. The king could not believe this and would not allow anyone to harm her. She, however, sat the whole time sewing the shirts and caring for nothing else.

The next time, when she again gave birth to a beautiful boy, the deceitful mother-in-law did the same thing, but the king could not bring himself to believe her accusations.

He said, "She is too pious and good to do anything like that. If she were not speechless, and if she could defend herself, her innocence would come to light."

But when the wicked mother stole away a newly born child for the third time and accused the queen, who did not defend herself with a single word, the king had no choice but to bring her to justice, and the queen was sentenced to die by fire.

When the day came for the sentence to be carried out, it was also the last day of the six years during which she had not been permitted to speak or to laugh, and she had thus delivered her dear brothers from the magic curse. The six shirts were finished. Only the left sleeve of the last one was missing. When she was led to the stake, she laid the shirts on her arm. Standing there, as the fire was about to be lit, she looked around, and six swans came flying through the air. When she saw that their redemption was near, her heart leaped with joy.

The swans rushed toward her, swooping down so that she could throw the shirts over them. As soon as the shirts touched them, their swan-skins fell off and her brothers stood before her in their bodies, vigorous and handsome. However, the youngest was missing his left arm. In its place, he had a swan's wing.

They embraced and kissed one another. Then the queen went to the king, who was greatly moved, and she began to speak, saying, "Dearest husband, now I may speak and reveal to you that I am innocent and falsely accused."

Then she told him of the treachery of the wicked mother-in-law who had taken away their three children and hidden them.

Then to the king's great joy, they were brought forth. As a punishment, the wicked mother-in-law was tied to the stake and burned to ashes. But the king and the queen with her six brothers lived many long years in happiness and peace.

The mother in our story has been betrayed and abandoned by her parents, and this has left her and her brothers vulnerable and unprotected. If you grew up experiencing emotional abandonment in childhood, it might make mothering more difficult. It is important that the heroine loses her brothers. Symbolically, this is an image of losing access to helpful energies in ourselves that could serve to support and enliven us. However, it could also have a more literal resonance. If we grow up in a family in which there is emotional abandonment or neglect, we may watch our siblings suffer as well. In families with absent or neglectful parents, older siblings often feel a great sense of responsibility for younger siblings and may take it upon themselves to protect them. This is an outsized responsibility to place on a child. In essence, the child has taken on an impossible task at which she will certainly fail, for no child can entirely replace a parent. This can create a lifelong burden of guilt as the older child watches her younger siblings grow up and struggle.

In the story, the heroine forfeits her voice to expiate the failings of her parents. Though the wounds were inflicted by the evil stepmother and the hapless king who failed to protect his children from his new wife, it is the daughter's sacrifice that is required. The sacrifice leaves her unable to express herself or protect her children.

The fairy tale is highlighting the ways in which we as mothers may struggle with difficult ancestral patterns of dysfunction. These legacies of harm can often be traced back through the generations and may affect us silently, without our conscious awareness. Becoming conscious of these ancient family patterns can go a long way toward redeeming the suffering of our ancestors and freeing ourselves and our children from these destructive legacies.

LOSING OUR VOICE

When the king's men find her in the tree, the heroine has no way to answer them other than to give away all of her jewelry and clothing. This is an image of psychic defenselessness. When we are in such a state, we may try to guarantee our safety by giving away what little we have, but this usually serves to make us more vulnerable. As women, we are especially prone to diminishing ourselves in an encounter with another person to communicate that we are not a threat.

When my daughter was a young teenager, I would often have occasion to overhear her conversations with her friends. I easily recognized the relational pattern typical among women—and especially among young women. The girls took turns putting themselves down. They did so in singsong chatter and often with nervous giggles. "I'm terrible at math, but then again, I'm terrible at just about every subject." "What is this thing my hair is doing today?" "God, I really suck at this game!" Though this is a common way for young women to talk, it was difficult to hear. Yet I appreciated that part of the function of this behavior was to communicate a kind of mutual nonaggression pact: I'm no threat to you; I'm not going to compete with you. When we are young and unsure of ourselves, sometimes making ourselves more vulnerable can serve its purpose—as it did for the princess in the fairy tale. The king is moved by her beauty and defenselessness and falls in love with her.

Of course, if overrelied upon, a relational strategy of constantly disarming and disrobing to escape conflict can make it difficult for us to ever claim any authority or to stand up for ourselves. As an occasional or temporary tactic, it has a place. However, when we are depressed or suffering from low self-worth, this may be our only defense—one that makes it difficult for us to protect ourselves or our children.

Much like the heroine in the tale, Rachel was courted by her husband for her beauty alone. She was silent in the sense that she hadn't found her voice. "I had no idea who I was," Rachel recalls.

Self-conscious about her accent and her lack of education, she remembers often making a conscious choice to stay silent at parties and social events in the days before her marriage. She realized early on that her job at such functions was to look beautiful. "Usually, if I just smiled a lot, that was good enough."

As mothers, we may be more susceptible to blocked care when we are like the fairy tale heroine. She is young, disenfranchised, and hasn't yet claimed her voice and authority. Rachel found herself thrust into a fast-paced adult world when she was still a teen. Her currency in that world was her beauty, and she had little chance to discover or develop other aspects of herself while she traded on it. She thus remained undeveloped and childlike. She had no experience with listening to and trusting herself by the time she had children. If you have never had the chance to develop a sense of agency, you may feel threatened and unsure when it comes time to care for children.

THE NEGATIVE MOTHER

It is significant that there is an evil mother-in-law in the tale. New mothers often experience a struggle with their mother-in-law over authority in caring for the child. My client Susan liked her mother-in-law very much and generally experienced her as warm and supportive. When she became a mother, however, she felt that her mother-in-law became possessive with the baby, often insisting that she be left alone with the child before Susan felt comfortable leaving him. When her mother-in-law joked that she "couldn't wait to get her hands on that baby," Susan did not find it at all funny. In my experience, Susan is hardly alone in having tension with her husband's mom in the early days of mothering. It is also common for grandmothers to feel that they know the right way to care for the baby and to be too heavy-handed when offering advice or "helping." This, of course, was also Rachel's experience. When her mother-in-law insisted on hiring people to care for the baby, Rachel did not have enough rootedness in her ground of being to contradict her.

Of course, Susan's mother-in-law wasn't "evil," and neither was Rachel's. The tale here is highlighting an archetypal pattern of a struggle between the generations as a younger woman is called to take her place as a mother and claim her authority, while the older woman must learn to cede control somewhat and make peace with her waning position. This rarely happens smoothly, as we see in Susan's and Rachel's stories—and plenty of TV sitcoms as well. When this intergenerational handoff does not go well—either because the younger woman has difficulty claiming authority or the older woman has trouble ceding it—this dynamic can contribute to blocked maternal care. Since it is vital that we as mothers feel competent in caring for our child in order to stay open and attached, when a mother-in-law undermines this sense of competence with too much criticism, interference, or "help," we may find it more difficult to connect.

We can also look at the figure of the mother-in-law symbolically, and it is here that her significance becomes most apparent. According to a psychological interpretation of the tale, the mother-in-law would represent an inner negative spoiling energy that takes away any new life the heroine brings forth. She would be an image of an internalized negative mother. All of us will have some version of an internalized negative mother, even if our own mother was loving and supportive. The inner energy can be a drain on our resources, causing us to question ourselves and feel inadequate. Your internalized negative mother may be especially potent if your actual mother was absent, depressed, critical, or emotionally or physically abusive.

When we have had damaging experiences in childhood with our parents, these become internalized and continue to affect us as adults. It is as if our early experience of our parents becomes the pattern for how we treat ourselves and how we unconsciously expect others to treat us. This may have a profound effect on our ability to advocate for ourselves, establish healthy relationships, and face adversity with resilience. Considered this way, both the stepmother and the mother-in-law in this tale are images of the heroine's mother—and the internalized negative mother that operates within her psyche.

We all internalize our parents as part of the natural development of our personality. We may literally have their voices in our heads—if we think about how we talk to ourselves and monitor the constant flow of inner dialogue, we are likely to recognize things that our parents used to tell us. This means that if our parents were able to comfort us when we were distressed, we would likely be able to draw on that experience as adults when facing adversity. Such an experience of positive mothering becomes an inner, inexhaustible resource. When we are upset, we can turn inward and find solace or at least the ability to be gentle with ourselves.

On the other hand, if our parents were distant, dismissive, contemptuous, or harshly critical, such a resource would be in short supply. Instead of finding comfort internally, we may have attacking inner voices that tell us we are no good. Having an internalized negative mother is very much like living with a curse, such as the one the brothers are under in this story. We may find it difficult to establish healthy relationships or pursue the things we want because some inner energy fills us with self-doubt or fear. "Hearing" daily in our heads that we are worthless or inadequate may make us depressed. We may choose to isolate ourselves in our fear that we won't be loved.

"The Six Swans" is a tale that concerns itself with the curse of a negative mother. The story begins with the children's father becoming lost in the forest—often a common image of the unconscious. With the father lost in an inner world, he is at the mercy of the witch and her scheme to marry him to her daughter. He is powerless to say no and marries the girl, even though he shudders when he sees her and fears that she will harm his children.

Women who have had adverse childhood experiences, such as parental abuse, are at a much higher risk of developing postpartum depression. Katherine Stone is a blogger and entrepreneur who suffered from debilitating postpartum anxiety. On her blog *Postpartum Progress*, she shares some of her story:

> When I was born I was placed for adoption. I lived with
> my adoptive parents for a few months—I don't even know
> how many, to be honest—and then was returned back to my
> biological parents, two young college students who hadn't
> planned on getting married or having a baby. I lived with
> parental alcoholism at a young age and also parental mental

> illness. It's no surprise to me, when I think about it, that
> I later suffered postpartum anxiety and OCD [obsessive
> compulsive disorder] after the birth of my first child.
>
> I was essentially hysterically vigilant over Jackson from
> the moment he was born. I worried I wouldn't be able to
> take care of him enough. I couldn't sleep. Couldn't relax.
> It felt very important to protect him, so much so that all
> of my intrusive thoughts were about me being the one to
> cause him hurt. I think now about the fact that my own
> experience in the first few unstable months of my life MUST
> have impacted how I was thinking and behaving when Jack
> was a newborn.[2]

If such negative, spoiling energies take up a lot of space in our psyche, they are likely to become activated when we become parents. For some of us, this may mean that we will suffer from a postpartum mood disorder. The image of the heroine voiceless, helpless to keep her babies from being taken away from her, looking to everyone as though she killed and ate them, is a striking and poignant psychological depiction of postpartum depression. Experts estimate that around 5 to 10 percent of moms suffer from postpartum depression in the weeks after giving birth. A much higher percentage of women will suffer from the less severe "postpartum blues." Symptoms of postpartum depression include having difficulty bonding with the baby, avoiding family or friends, and experiencing intrusive thoughts of harming the child—all of which our heroine seems to be exhibiting. (We can understand her blood-smeared mouth as an image of her fear that she might hurt her children.)

ISOLATION AND DESPAIR

When substance abuse, depression, stress, or other issues make it difficult for us to feel open and relaxed to the experience of motherhood, the result can be blocked care. This experience can bring deep shame as we find ourselves feeling unthinkable things—that we don't like being a mother or wish we hadn't had children. These are feelings that cannot be easily shared or spoken about and so can be profoundly isolating. In extreme cases, these feelings can lead to a permanent disconnection from ourselves and our children of the most brutal kind.

American poet and novelist Sylvia Plath is an example of a woman whose struggle with depression rendered her, in the end, mute and helpless to protect herself or her children. Plath's father died when she was eight, leaving her with a difficult emotional inheritance. She battled depression throughout her young life, attempting suicide at age twenty. Her marriage to British poet Ted Hughes seemed at first to bring the possibility of great happiness. However, when he left her for another woman the same year her second child was born, Plath fell into a deep depression. Like the heroine in "The Six Swans," Plath had limited resources to help her cope with her isolation and despair. In wintry London, she was alone and far from home. Though she made determined efforts to find help, she wasn't able to stay connected to herself and her children. On February 11, 1963, Plath placed wet towels along the doorjambs in the kitchen to keep the CO_2 gas from leaking into the room next door where her toddler and infant lay sleeping, then killed herself by putting her head in the oven. Plath's tragic story amplifies one way of considering the plight of our fairy-tale mother, whose depletion and silence left her unable to show up for her children.

In the tale, the process of recovery from the spell takes six years of tedious, exacting work. For six years, the heroine does little else other than sew the shirts that will bring her brothers' deliverance. This is analogous to the hard work that one must undertake to recover from childhood trauma or emotional abuse. It may take us years to break the spell. This often involves knitting together a new internal sense of safety by purposely cultivating gentleness and compassion toward ourselves. As we continue our journey down the well, there will be opportunities for such healing. In subsequent sections of this book, we will learn more about how to break such spells—and the benefits of doing so.

Sylvia Plath and Rachel are both extreme examples of disconnection, but we likely all felt some degree of abandonment in childhood that can prime us to pull away from our children when we ourselves become parents. It may be that your parents were overly invested in work, or perhaps there was a divorce. Maybe you came from a family where it seemed as though there weren't ever enough emotional resources to go around. All of these kinds of experiences can make it difficult for us to hold on to ourselves as we parent. Motherhood will give us the opportunity to revisit these wounds and possibly heal them.

BREAKING THE SPELL

My client Olive was the oldest child in a family where both of her parents were alcoholics. She grew up in an atmosphere of chaos and even occasional violence. She recalls that her father would often become rageful after he had been drinking, and she remembers hiding with her younger siblings in her bedroom to escape his fury. By the time Olive was a teen, she was drinking heavily. A hard worker and talented student, she put herself through college by bartending—work that covered her expenses but made continued drinking easier. By the time she graduated, she was in a serious relationship with a man who was also an alcoholic. When she became pregnant a few years later, the two married. Shortly afterward, the couple had a second child.

Today, Olive tears up as she recalls her early years of parenting. Blackout drinking was a weekly occurrence, and she has few memories of her children's early years. She does remember feeling easily annoyed by her children and wanting to avoid them whenever possible. She routinely let her husband watch the kids so that she could go out drinking with friends. She knows that she was frequently irritable with her children and experienced them as burdensome. There were significant tensions in her marriage from the earliest days, and she and her husband often fought loudly in front of the kids. When her husband became violent toward her, Olive had the resilience and fortitude to take the children and leave him. For several years after the divorce, she continued to drink actively, functioning well enough to hold down a job and manage the basics of parenting, but not really able to connect with either herself and her own needs—or her children.

One night, she got so drunk that she passed out in an alley and woke up alone in the early morning. This event was for her the moment of "hitting bottom"—she went to an Alcoholics Anonymous

(AA) meeting the next day and has been sober since. Olive came to see me just a few months after she quit drinking. While we focused on many different issues together, part of the work Olive had to do was to come to learn who she was and what really mattered to her. While she was drinking, she was never able to feel her feelings. She used alcohol and compulsive work to stuff her emotions. Getting sober was a slow process of learning about herself and her needs, a process made all the more difficult due to the young age at which she had started drinking.

A related part of her process was connecting with her children. This involved forgiving herself for not being the mother she wished she had been when her children were younger. It required her to drop out of compulsive doing so that she could attune to them and enjoy being with them. These things took time. Eventually, Olive felt competent at meeting both her children's material and emotional needs.

During one session, she shared with me an experience she had had in a recent AA meeting. A woman had told her story. This woman drank throughout her children's childhood and only became sober once they were adults. The woman expressed deep grief over the time she had missed. Olive was able to feel great empathy with this woman. She could also feel gratitude that she had stopped drinking while her children were young. She had many years ahead to parent, connect with, and enjoy her children.

The tale tells us that the children who had been taken away were reunited with their parents after the mother-in-law's treachery is revealed. Occasional disruptions in our connection with our kids are normal. The bonds between a mother and her children are strong and elastic. They can be stretched a great deal and then snap right back into place. Even years of blocked care can be healed and repaired, as was true for Olive. However, if our ability to connect with ourselves and our children is chronically impaired for a long time, some losses may be permanent, as was true for Rachel.

Any substantial loss will need to be mourned. Olive had to grieve the lost years of infancy and early childhood for which she was not present. Those years were gone, part of the unchangeable past. Rachel had more losses to comes to terms with, and this task was at the center of our work. Rachel was asked to mourn the relationships with her children that she had never had. This required her to move out of self-blame, which keeps us stuck. She had to find forgiveness and acceptance for the person she had been. Then there were many tears to be shed.

Questions for Reflection for Losing Ourselves

1. When have you felt disconnected from yourself? From your children? What is this like for you when you feel this way?

2. The fairy tale in this chapter begins when the king becomes lost in the forest and is therefore susceptible to the witch's ploy to get him to marry her daughter. Where in your life have you felt that you had lost your way in a dark wood? How did you manage to find your way out?

3. The heroine in the story has a stepmother who wishes her harm and a father who is unable to protect her. Most of us come to adulthood with some wounds from childhood—even those of us with "good enough" parents. These wounds can become especially activated when we become parents. In what ways were you unprotected or wounded in childhood?

4. The heroine is unable to defend herself since she cannot speak. Defenseless, she responds by giving away what she has when she first meets the king's men. When have you found that you have lost your voice—your ability to speak up for yourself and your needs? How did you respond?

5. In the tale, the heroine's mother-in-law steals away the babies. As a mother, who or what has momentarily stolen away your connection with your maternal authority by encouraging you to doubt yourself?

6. The image of a young woman who cannot laugh or speak and whose babies get taken away from her is a poignant

metaphor for feelings of depression that may visit us when we are mothers. Revisit your answer to question 1 above and the times you have felt disconnected from yourself and your children. In the fairy tale, this disconnection lasts for years. Moments of feeling disconnected from our children are normal, though difficult to speak about. What factors contribute to your becoming periodically disconnected from your children?

7. The heroine in the tale is able to restore her connection to her children when she is able to redeem her brothers. Doing so has taken years of painstaking work. When you have felt disconnected from your own source and/or cut off from your feelings for your children, what work have you had to do to restore connection?

8. What issues from your childhood have resurfaced for you after you became a mother?

PART II

AT THE BOTTOM

CHAPTER 4

Encountering Darkness

If there is anything that we wish to change in our children,
we should first examine it and see whether it is not
something that could better be changed in ourselves.

C. G. JUNG
COLLECTED WORKS, VOL. 17

The heroine in "The Two Caskets" takes a difficult and frightening plunge into the well and finds herself in a strange land. There she encounters fences, ovens, and cows that speak. She finds helpful animals and an odd old woman who sets her difficult tasks. Many myths and fairy tales tell of strange adventures and challenging trials in a subterranean land. The Sumerian goddess Inanna journeyed to the underworld to visit her sister and was killed and hung on a meat peg to rot; Psyche had to visit Hades to retrieve some of Persephone's beauty before she could be reunited with Eros, her beloved husband. The mythologist Joseph Campbell noted that hero stories usually involve a visit to the abyss where the protagonist must face a frighten-ing ordeal. Whenever a motif frequently occurs across the centuries and continents, we know that it has universal relevance for the human condition. In other words, it is archetypal.

As we mother, we will encounter ordeals and trials no less daunting than that of the mythic heroines. One of those trials will likely involve us meeting those aspects of ourselves that are off-putting, regrettable, or even disgusting and repulsive. Encountering the parts of ourselves we would rather not acknowledge is a necessary aspect of psychological growth. We are most likely to notice these parts of ourselves by first noticing them in other people, seeing our most despised qualities as belonging to those around us. If we have children, we will inevitably project our worst qualities onto them. All parents at one time or another see the most despised parts of themselves carried by their children. If we can stay in relationship with our children when this happens, we will have the opportunity to get to know and accept the least likable parts of ourselves—the parts that Jung referred to as our shadow.

SHADOW

Jung once defined the shadow as "the thing [a person] has no wish to be."[1] It is a collection of the unacceptable aspects of our nature that were cast into the dark in the process of personality development. From our parents, teachers, and culture we learned what parts of ourselves needed to be hidden. Anger, selfishness, and sexuality are some examples of those aspects of ourselves that we may have learned to think of as unacceptable. Your family may have had their own particular "rules" about what was acceptable. For example, you may have learned it wasn't okay to be boastful, artistic, intellectual, or any other number of qualities. Chances are, you learned to split off these parts of yourself and banish them into the unconscious so that you didn't have to admit that you had these qualities. But eventually we come to meet these split-off parts of ourselves at some point in our lives. Then they must be reckoned with.

The confrontation with the shadow is the first step on the difficult journey to individuation, or that process by which we become who we were meant to be. While certain shadow qualities can be recognized and dealt with fairly easily, others may be more difficult for us to see and acknowledge. For example, I may be able to see my tendency toward overindulgence—it might be hard to miss as I notice my weight creep up! It might be harder for me to admit to myself that I feel profoundly inadequate and shame-filled at times, in spite of a competent persona that I present to the world. Those aspects of ourselves that are least acceptable to the ego are usually only experienced in projection, meaning that we see these qualities in other people and are sure that they belong to someone other than ourselves.

My daughter was five when I took the comprehensive exams as part of my training to become an analyst. On a day in late December, I strapped the kids in their car seats and ran back inside to get a crate full of books. I was going to my parents for the day to read. Studying had not been going well. Whenever I looked at the material, I felt hopelessly inadequate. I had had a dream the previous night in which I was talking to one of my clients, complaining that I hadn't accomplished much in my life. I woke up feeling irritable and restless. I popped the trunk and slung the crate of books in it.

It was warm for December, and a young boy about my daughter's age pedaled down the sidewalk in front of our house on his two-wheeler. I felt an immediate stab of discomfort and self-doubt. My daughter had gotten a "big girl" bike for her last birthday six months ago. She not only couldn't ride it yet but also showed no interest in learning—in fact, she was afraid to try. I spent the hour's drive worrying about all the ways that she was potentially behind her peers. I felt annoyed with myself, but also with her. Why couldn't she be advanced, like some of the other kids I knew? It was only hours later that I recognized that I was projecting my concerns about myself onto her. As in Jung's quote at the beginning of this chapter, what I wished to change in my daughter was, in fact, something that needed to be addressed within myself.

PROJECTING DISOWNED
PARTS OF OURSELVES

According to Jung, "Everything that irritates us about others can lead us to an understanding of ourselves."[2] In other words, one good way to find out which qualities you might be projecting is to identify that person who most annoys you, who most gets under your skin. What about that person irks you the most? It is likely to be that quality that you have repudiated in yourself. I once worked with a woman named Ellen, whom I could not abide. Ellen was pretty, and she knew it. She flirted easily and loved being the center of attention. It was obvious that she thought she was pretty fabulous. When I was growing up, claiming the spotlight and feeling pretty fabulous were considered to be highly inappropriate. Those feelings were in the shadow for me, so seeing Ellen live them out really made me hate her!

Jung pointed out that there is always a "hook" for projections. Ellen really was a little conceited. If she hadn't had that quality, my projection wouldn't have had a place to land. But my irritation with her far outstripped anyone else's. It had much more energy than called for by the situation. My greatly disproportionate response to her self-importance was a clue to me that projection of my own material was involved. Just because we find someone irritating or off-putting doesn't always mean that we are projecting our shadow onto that person, but if we find we are having an outsized reaction, it ought to make us curious.

Fairy tales can help illustrate the different kinds of material we project, what we do with these projections, and the outcome for ourselves and our children. If we permanently burden our children with the job of carrying those qualities of ours that we deem unacceptable, we condemn our children to a lifetime's work trying to separate themselves from our projections. At the same time, we lose the opportunity to get to know ourselves better since we never learn that the projected qualities belong to us. The Grimm's tale "The Raven" depicts a mother who wishes her daughter would just fly away—or, in other words, carry away the mother's shadow. The mother's wish comes true and thus she bewitches her infant daughter. Here's how the story begins:

Once upon a time, a queen had a little daughter. One day, the child was naughty, and the mother could not get her to quiet down. The queen became impatient. At that moment, she saw ravens flying about the palace. She opened the window and said, "I wish you were a raven and would fly away from here! Then I would be able to get some rest." The moment she spoke these words, the child changed into a raven and flew from her arms out of the window. It flew into a dark forest and stayed there for a long time, and the parents heard nothing of their child.

The moment the queen becomes impatient, shadow stuff is "out there," flying around. When her shadow stuff flies around, she wishes it upon her little daughter. It is as if the queen has said, "I wish you would carry my shadow and take it far away from here," and simply wishing makes it so. Poignantly, the tale gives the impression that neither the king nor the queen tries to rescue their daughter. Like many parents, they are satisfied to let the child carry the shadow, finding her a convenient scapegoat.

When we become impatient with our children, it can be as if they are momentarily changed into something else with which we have little relationship. In fact, like the mother in the fairy tale, we have effected this change by projecting our disagreeable qualities onto our children. When I am having trouble tolerating some part of myself, or when I am afraid that I am inadequate or unlovable and not fully conscious of these feelings, I project these unacceptable qualities onto my child. In the story, the pronoun used to refer to the princess is "it" after the mother curses her child. When we use our children to help us feel better about ourselves by asking them to be the carriers of our own rejected qualities, we deprive them of their full humanness. If we are too deeply unconscious about this process, it constitutes a kind of trauma that exiles an essential part of our child's soul to the dark forest of the unconscious. And we as mothers lose an opportunity for greater self-knowledge.

Projection is an entirely normal process that we all unconsciously engage in frequently, and all parents will inevitably project aspects of themselves onto their children. Our children will likely carry for us at one time or another the most despised and rejected parts of ourselves. If we have always struggled to stay thin and our child is gaining weight, we might react to this with outsized shame or horror. If we have been shy and introverted our whole life, we might cringe to watch our child hover close to the wall at a birthday party. If we've always suffered from feelings of inadequacy, our child's underachievement might bring up big feelings of rage, anxiety, or sadness. We will surely sometimes find that we don't like aspects of our children. If we can gain consciousness about our reactions, we will often find that these disagreeable traits are our disowned and projected qualities. The crucial question is whether we can become aware that we have projected our shadows onto our children.

When we project our shadow material onto our children without becoming conscious that we are doing so, it can poison their lives. It is a spell they must break, and doing so often comes at a great cost. The 1980 film *Ordinary People* illustrates this dynamic. The film begins a few weeks after Conrad Jarrett, a high school student in a Chicago suburb, has come home from an extended stay at a psychiatric hospital following a suicide attempt. As the movie unfolds, we learn that Conrad became depressed and suicidal after surviving a boating accident in which his older brother, Buck, was killed. Buck was the family star and his mother's favorite child. While we are not told much about Conrad's relationship with his mother before Buck's death, we learn that she has never been close to Conrad. It is likely that Conrad has always been the recipient of her shadow projections—he was not the star swimmer that his brother was—but after Buck's death, Conrad carries her grief and depression as well.

The brittle Mrs. Beth Jarrett is unable to grieve her son's death. She is so cut off from her authentic feelings that she does not cry at the funeral. During the film, we see her anxious to leave her son's death behind. She urges her husband to plan a trip to Europe so that they can "get back to normal." When we as mothers have a hard time allowing ourselves to feel our authentic emotions, we may be tempted to hide behind our persona.

Jung defined persona to mean the mask that we wear out in the world. Everyone needs a persona, perhaps even several, depending on the roles we need to fill. Although a persona is always somewhat superficial, it is important and healthy to have one. A persona is only a problem in terms of psychological health when we are too rigidly identified with it—when we cannot take off the mask. Beth is completely identified with her persona. She is focused on tennis and golf, as well as social engagements and cocktail parties. Even at a time of great grief, she is preoccupied with a persona issue. Her husband, Calvin, confronts her about the fact that she was worried about the shoes he was wearing to their son's funeral. Being so identified with this upbeat persona, she is unable to let in the dark side—her shadow—that would compensate that persona.

Shadow material is particularly threatening to those with narcissistic traits, such as Beth. The narcissist is primarily interested in others for how they can support the narcissist's self-esteem. As a defense against her own feelings of shame or inadequacy, the narcissistic mother may identify with how she wishes to see herself and need to see that reflected around her in her home and her children. The shadow material that could "challenge us, penetrate our defenses, and lead us into further development"[3] is unable to be tolerated because it could undermine the idealized way we want others to see us. Beth was able to identify with Buck because he reflected how she would like to be perceived. He was the star of the swim team. Conrad has failed her in this regard. (That it was problematic for Buck to be a narcissistic extension of his mother is implied in the irony of his death—the star swimmer drowned.)

Beth's depression and despair are in the shadow because they are not socially acceptable in her country-club life. Conrad's suicide attempt was messy and embarrassing to her, as Conrad explains to his psychiatrist during a session: "Listen, I'm never gonna be forgiven for that. Never! You know, you can't get it out, you know, all the blood in her towels, in her rug. Everything had to be pitched. Even the tiles in the bathroom had to be regrouted."[4]

All of the grief that she has been unable to feel is projected onto Conrad, who carries it for her. Like most who carry a shadow, he is ostracized and rejected for doing so. Beth can barely stand to be around her son because he is everything she doesn't want to be. His interactions with his mother are tense and awkward, laced with venomous anger and rejection on her part that simmer right below the surface. Her visible antipathy for him is fueled by the disowned and projected grief that he carries for her. She would like to get rid of him. Beth discusses sending Conrad away to boarding school because he "provokes people," just as the biblical scapegoat is cast out into the desert carrying the sins of the tribe, as described in the Hebrew Bible's book of Leviticus.

RECLAIMING AND INTEGRATING SHADOW

But what about the mother who is able to stay in some sort of relationship with the disowned part of herself? After all, projecting shadow material is normal. All mothers project their shadow onto their children, and yet all children do not suffer like Conrad or the princess-turned-raven. When we can accept and reclaim those repudiated parts of ourselves, we will find that meeting our shadow can become an opportunity for significant growth.

Motherhood provides a wonderful opportunity for confronting shadow projections because it can be difficult to maintain these negative projections on those we love so much, feel so responsible for, and identify with to such a degree. It can be hard to stay split, not least because when we find our children to be objectionable, we often must admit that we have played either a genetic or behavioral role in shaping their actions. Where this happens, the shadow projection rebounds back to us, accounting in part for the intensity of the experience of motherhood. As long as we are not too closed and unconscious, we won't be able to help but be witness to our shadows.

When we can welcome with compassion what is most despised in ourselves and our children, this material can be transformed. Motherhood may provide a redemptive opportunity to reclaim cast-off parts of ourselves because we are able to relate to our shadow material more compassionately when we see it carried by our children. Moreover, we may be motivated by the depth of our love for our children to move beyond our self-loathing and shame and come to terms with our shadow. We can then mother ourselves in such a way that we accept what is most detestable in ourselves. We are then open to relate to others with real intimacy. When we can accept our flawed self, then we are more likely to be caring and accepting of those we love as well.

The Sierra Leonean fairy tale "The Story of Two Women" beautifully illustrates the transformative potential of accepting shadow material and how doing so is crucial to becoming generative.

THE STORY OF TWO WOMEN

Once there were two wives married to the same man. Neither of them had been able to bear children, and they both greatly desired to do so. One day, a man passing through the village told of an old woman nearby who knew the medicine for having children. The first wife went right away to the old woman and beseeched her to help her bear a child.

The old woman said, "Will you wash off its filth?" "Yes." "Will you allow it to wet on you?" "Yes." "Will you be able to be vomited on?" "Yes." "Will you like the vomit?" "Yes." "Well, sit down." The woman sat down. She had food cooked for her. She finished eating. The night came, and the old woman told the first wife to get into bed.

"Whatever comes to you here, if you want to bear children—don't be afraid! Treat the thing well." The first wife agreed. In the middle of the night, a great snake slithered up to the young woman. She was afraid, but she calmed herself and welcomed the snake. As soon as she did so, the snake transformed into a little pillow. The young woman took the pillow gently, kissed it three times, and laid her head on it.

A little while later, rats came. They began to pee on her, but she didn't mind. She didn't worry about getting pee on her fine clothes.

In the morning, the old woman came and saw what had happened and was pleased. Without the young girl seeing her, she took a basket and placed in it a baby girl whose body was covered with sores. She also placed in the basket medicine to heal the sores. She gave the basket to the first wife along with the medicine for having children.

"Don't open the basket until you are by the water," said the old woman. "When you reach there, cook some rice and then open the basket. Take the medicine for having children with the rice."

The young woman did as the old woman had instructed her. When she had finished cooking the rice, she opened the basket and found the sore-covered child. She lifted the child out carefully, placed her on her knee, and kissed her repeatedly. She found the medicine to heal the sores, bathed the child, and rubbed the ointment on her sores. Then she fed the child some rice, and the child was cured.

The first wife returned to her village, where she continued to care for the girl, and she also bore a boy child soon after.

Now the second wife saw this and wanted to know how to bear a child. She asked the first wife how she had done it, and the first wife told her all. The second wife was the more beloved one between the two. She always had the most beautiful clothes made from expensive fabrics. She now went to the old woman with the medicine for having children and told her that she desired to bear a child.

The old woman said, "I have something to ask you. Can you wash off the filth?" The second wife said, "What! I didn't come here to wash off filth. Look at me and my beautiful clothes. Don't ask me that again!" Then the old woman said, "Will you be able to wash off pee?" The second wife was outraged, "Stop this! I did not come here to you for you to go and ask me to wash off pee!" Then the old woman said, "Will you agree to be vomited on? Will you wash off the vomit?" Then she said, "I won't answer such a question! You are only saying such things because you are so old."

Just as she had done for the first wife, the old woman showed her to bed and told her to welcome whatever came to her in the night. But when the snake came, the second wife threw it done and struck it dead. When the rats came, she stood up and shrieked that their pee was spoiling her fine clothes.

In the morning, the old woman came and saw what had happened. But she wasn't unfair. She gave the same thing to the second wife that she had given to the first. She likewise told the second wife not to open the basket until she had reached the water. But the second wife didn't listen. She didn't trust the old woman, and she opened the basket on the road and peeped in. There she saw a shiny skin—a snake! She closed the basket and continued, and when she reached the water, she cooked her rice and opened the basket again.

This time she found in the basket a sore-covered child. She took some rags and rammed them in the child's mouth so that the child wouldn't cry. She did not want people to know that she had brought back a child covered with sores. She walked straight back to the old woman's house, dropped the basket, and said angrily, "I did not come to you to beg a child with sores." and when she returned to her village, she died.

Just as we saw in the tale of "The Two Caskets," the two wives illustrate different ways of relating to the unconscious. In this case, we might say that they show two manners of being with our real and inner children. We all have within us a shadow child covered in sores, who may be painful or difficult for us to see. In the crucible of motherhood, we are likely to meet that child. The fairy tale teaches us that, to be life-giving, we must be able to love her. The second wife is too identified with her persona—her fine, expensive clothes—to be able to accept the sore-covered child. She is worried about what others might think. Psychic death and sterility are the result. The second wife does not understand that to be fertile and generative, she must open herself up to that which is disgusting and repulsive—that which has been disowned.

The goal of alchemy was to produce the elusive, miraculous substance sometimes referred to as the "philosopher's stone." The alchemists said of this most precious of all things that it is found in "loathsome filth" and is "cast upon the dung heap."[5] So within the reviled shadow material lies the great treasure. The first wife behaves like an alchemist, welcoming the snake and the peeing rats so that they transform, and nurturing the baby in the basket.

SNAKE WISDOM

The snake is a highly complex and varied symbol. Since the snake transforms itself into the sore-covered child, we know that it is associated with the child in our story. In certain cultures, the snake has been identified with fertility, sexuality, and specifically pregnancy. The Italian fairy tale "Biancabella and the Snake" begins with a queen who is unable to conceive until, during a nap in the garden, a little grass snake crawls under her clothes, penetrates her, and rests in her womb. The presence of the snake in this sense seems to be saying that you cannot conceive a new life without being in touch with the instincts, which the snake represents. Conception, of course, requires one to be sexually active. In "The Story of the Two Women," it is as if the second wife would rather not bother with these dirty, carnal things. She does not want to know the snake of sexual passion and instinct. She would prefer not to be penetrated by this energy.

Those who would prefer to avoid the shadow side do not recognize that new life requires that we get down in shadowy, bodily stuff and get dirty. Because the instinctual aspects of life are defended against, they appear threatening. The serpent is also associated with the lower psyche, the realm of mysterious bodily processes. When we become pregnant, our bodies begin a miraculous undertaking of knitting up a new human life. This strange event takes place within our body but far from our conscious awareness. It is a process that is directed by the unfathomable depths of the autonomic nervous system. Our body proceeds to create this life without any input from consciousness, with primitive snakelike wisdom that is awe-inspiring, mysterious, and utterly foreign to conscious life. It can be difficult for some of us to trust this process when we are pregnant.

The first snake in the story transforms itself into a pillow when welcomed and loved. Jung said that the unconscious "reflects the face we turn toward it. Hostility lends it a threatening aspect, friendliness softens its features."[6] If we defend and revile our shadow, what looks back to us is frightening, disgusting, and seemingly worthless. If we can approach the unconscious with open curiosity, we will find it a helpful friend. A pillow provides comfort. It is associated with our most personal thoughts and secrets—our private inner life. It is where we lay our heads to sleep and dream. When welcomed, the snake goes from being somewhat frightening and potentially threatening to supportive and comforting, especially as regards our inner life.

A woman in the last days of her third pregnancy had the following dream that relates to some of the themes explored above.

> *I was at the hospital when a nurse came in and put the baby*
> *in my arms. There was a bathing tub where childbirth would*
> *happen. The water was clean. Suddenly we saw a snake moving*
> *in the bathing tub. First it was flat and transparent, but soon*
> *it was hard and coiled. I thought this was interesting because I*
> *compared it with the movements of the baby inside my womb.*
> *The other people were frightened and wanted to kill the snake.*
> *Tranquil and without fear I told them it was going away and*
> *would not harm anyone.[7]*

The dreamer correctly intuits that a hostile approach to the snake is not the one required. It must be met calmly and without fear. As with our fairy tale, the snake is associated with the child. It is in the water where the birth will take place, and the dreamer suggests that the fetal movements in utero were snakelike. Interestingly, a few weeks after this dream, the dreamer underwent a Cesarean section, and it was found that the umbilical cord was wrapped twice around the baby's neck. The baby was delivered unharmed.

In "Biancabella and the Snake," a queen who has been unable to become pregnant at last conceives a daughter when a little snake enters her. The baby is born with a grass snake wrapped three times around her neck. In the tale, those assisting at the birth are very frightened, but the snake gently unwinds itself from the infant's neck and slithers away into the garden. The midwives then notice a beautiful gold necklace around the baby's neck. Like the umbilical cord, the snake is both the giver of all nurture and life and the potential cause of strangulation and death. The snake is associated with the creation of new life and with death, with the cycle of life and death and with rebirth. To have access to the life force, we as mothers must be in touch with serpent energy—that which relates to the primordial creation-destruction cycle. The fairy tale suggests that we must be willing to welcome death to welcome life.

ACCEPTING OUR CHILDREN—AND OURSELVES

In "The Story of Two Women," the old woman gives the wife both a sore-covered child and the medicine to heal the sores. So too, our psyches hold wounds and the balm to heal these wounds. When we can nurture our inner sore-covered child and allow her to transform, we will have prepared the way to nurture another. Our real, outer children will have sores. Loving our children in a deeply connected way rather than using them to regulate our narcissistic needs requires profound acceptance of their sores and our own. Accepting our children offers opportunities for us to accept ourselves more fully as well. Accepting what is messy, untamed, and undesirable in your children is about accepting those messy children in your own soul who may never before have received love or acceptance.

Cassie sought therapy with me to address growing feelings of depression. Cassie was a statuesque, elegant, beautiful woman who dressed impeccably and presented a polished, sophisticated persona to the world. She worked as an executive in the fashion industry, so her attention to her appearance served her well in her professional life. Cassie had always been professionally ambitious and successful. Her elder daughter, who was likewise stunning and fashionable, seemed to be following in her footsteps and was on track to attend a prestigious college. However, Cassie was worried about her younger daughter, Helena, who was in middle school when Cassie first contacted me.

Cassie explained that Helena had always danced to her own tune, preferring as a child to play dolls by herself in her room when the rest of the family preferred more extraverted pursuits. Whereas Cassie's older daughter had been interested in wearing pretty clothes from an early age, Helena was always pleasantly oblivious about matters of appearance. As Helena entered puberty, she began to gain weight. Cassie quickly mobilized to help Helena stay slim, but Helena was resistant to her efforts. It was around this time that Cassie began noticing that she frequently felt lethargic and tearful.

When she first came to see me, Cassie noted with considerable discomfort that she was not just concerned for Helena's health—she was ashamed of her. She first reached out to me after attending a mother-daughter function at school. Cassie was horrified to notice her annoyance and even disgust with her daughter in comparison with Helena's thinner, more accomplished peers. I expressed acceptance of Cassie's unthinkable thoughts about her daughter and suggested that we might become curious about them.

As Cassie and I explored the depression that seemed to have settled in her as she watched Helena's weight creep up, memories from her adolescence surfaced. She, too, had been introverted like Helena, but her family had been harshly critical of this trait. Cassie's father was an iron-fisted tyrant who required that his very idiosyncratic rules be followed. Spending time alone in her room during the daytime, for example, was prohibited. She recalled that she had always been heavy as a child, and her father had criticized her for that as well. As she entered puberty, she had noticeably gained weight—and the whole family had pointed this out to her with concern. It was around this time that her father precipitously left the family. His sudden disappearance threw the family into financial chaos and was traumatic for everyone.

Cassie remembers her life as being split into a "before" and "after" her father's disappearance. After her father left, she became out of necessity a self-reliant little adult. She became a perfectionistic student and rose to the top of her class. She began dieting and exercising with religious zeal. Cassie and I came to see that these behaviors were adaptations that warded of intolerable feelings of vulnerability and helplessness. These adaptations had proven useful in helping her to manage her chaotic adolescence, and they had continued to be useful into adulthood, where her glamorous persona and achievement orientation allowed her to excel in her line of work. However, these strategies required that the heavy little girl who enjoyed getting lost in her fantasies be buried and forgotten. This shadow part of her remained cut off from conscious awareness—until Helena reached puberty.

Together, we noted that Cassie's depressive symptoms began when Helena turned thirteen—the same age that Cassie had been when her father left. Cassie began to see that her sometimes intensely negative feelings toward Helena were really due to her shadow self being projected onto her child. Helena then became the sore-covered child that the second wife in the fairy tale wanted to reject. Cassie was able to soften into compassion—for Helena, but importantly also for her adolescent self, who had had to go underground when her father left.

Cassie was able to drop into the grief she had not been able to feel previously over the sudden end of her childhood. Over time, Cassie's depressive symptoms abated. Her concerns over Helena's weight eased. Without her mother's ferocious attention on her weight and her body, Helena was able to more or less regulate her weight by herself. I noted that Cassie became somewhat more relaxed in her appearance and grooming. She was still elegant and attractive, but her manner of dress grew more casual and less controlled. One day she confessed to me that she had been enjoying weekend afternoons reading alone in her bedroom—something she had not let herself do in many years. It was as if she had been reintroduced to her shadow qualities by meeting them in her daughter. Now she was able to fully embrace these formerly rejected parts of herself, creating new channels through which her life energy could flow.

Cassie had been embarrassed to admit that she found her daughter shameful, and yet disclosing these feelings to me had begun the process of accepting both herself and her child. In the course of parenting our children, there will certainly be times that we are disappointed, ashamed, and even disgusted by them. When these feelings seem particularly strong or difficult to bear, we may be sure that some of the "heat" in these reactions comes from our having projected our most hated aspects of self onto our children. Though this is uncomfortable—and can become a lifelong burden to our children if we don't do our work—such feelings can also help us open to those parts of ourselves we had to split off for one reason or another. The shameful, reviled contents that our children may carry for us can be great teachers if we can turn to face them and see that they are really ours.

Questions for Reflection
for Encountering Darkness

1. What in your child irritates you the most? Or makes you most ashamed? If your reaction to these qualities seems out of proportion, these may be projected shadow qualities. How does that seem to fit?

2. The woman who has the medicine for having children asks the first wife right away whether she will be willing to clean up filth, pee, and vomit. Did you have to overcome any serious doubts or misgivings before embracing becoming a mother? If so, what was this like?

3. In "The Story of Two Women," the process of becoming pregnant involves welcoming the snake and the rats. It often is the case that pregnancy exposes us to aspects of our physicality we may not have spent much time thinking

about before. We become aware of our bodies in a new way. This might mean overcoming disgust or squeamishness about our bodily processes. If you became a mother through birth, what was your experience with pregnancy like in this regard? What did you have to welcome that would otherwise have disgusted or alarmed you, either physically or psychologically?

4. Sometimes it is easier for us to treat those shameful aspects of ourselves with greater kindness when we meet them first in our children. When has your child evidenced a quality you might normally feel ashamed of but you were instead able to relate to with loving care?

5. Proper care of the sore-covered child is evidently crucial for a happy outcome in the story. Where is your sore-covered child—a part of you that is hidden and of which perhaps you are ashamed? In what ways recently have you treated that part of yourself with kindness, soothing it, and treating it with medicine?

6. The second wife is too concerned with her fine clothes to be able to receive the snake, the rats, or the sore-covered child. We all have times when we are unable to be open to our inner sore-covered children. For some of us, doing so might be quite difficult. In what ways recently have you treated that part of yourself harshly, by stuffing its face with rags?

7. The second wife is repulsed by the sore-covered child. There will inevitably be times when our children do things that we find embarrassing, shameful, or even disgusting. When recently have you felt shame or disgust in reaction to something your child did? How did you respond to this?

8. What parts of yourself are you particularly ashamed of? What have you split off?

CHAPTER 5

Valuing Darkness

The shadow is a tight passage, a narrow door,
whose painful constriction no one is spared
who goes down to the deep well.

C. G. JUNG
COLLECTED WORKS, VOL. 9

When we find ourselves at the bottom of the well, we will be tested. Through the trials of motherhood, you may encounter aspects of yourself that surprise you. In this way, your children can be your teachers, leading you into relationship with forgotten or disowned parts of yourself. Much of what got buried or hidden in the process of ego and persona development may have been instincts, abilities, and qualities that were deemed unacceptable for some reason. But these aspects of ourselves have tremendous energy attached to them and could be sources of potential renewal for us later in life. Jung referred to these qualities as the positive shadow—latent potentials within us that have been left languishing. Sometimes it will be the case that what our children carry for us will be valuable parts of ourselves that we, for whatever reason, have been unable to claim. If we as mothers find our child living out these qualities, we may have a range of reactions. If these qualities are too unconscious for us and therefore threatening, we may find them very difficult to tolerate in our child. We may have envy that our child can live out some aspect of our personality that we were forced to disown. Or we may find that we can come into relationship with these qualities through first meeting them externally in our child.

Your children may hold for you some quality that is still in your shadow, such as assertiveness, free-spiritedness, joyful sexuality, or creativity. If you were not allowed to live these qualities, you might be committed to permitting your children to live them. Long before we feel entitled to claim these qualities for ourselves, we may be able to claim them for our children, thereby possibly paving the way for our future change of personality.

WHAT WENT UNDERGROUND

My client Selene was a bright, spirited child who was subjected to persistent emotional and physical abuse by her mother. Selene's adult daughter Katie carries latent potentials that Selene was for a long time unable to see as her own. "Katie wasn't easygoing all the time like her older brother," Selene says. "She was a real spitfire! Katie is a better version of me. She's what I would have been if I had had a decent mother. She lights up a room when she walks in, and she doesn't take shit from anyone. She can stand up for herself. She's outgoing and has a lot of friends."

Forced to be compliant in an attempt to mitigate her mother's rages and get whatever love and approval may have been available, Selene had to hide away her natural feistiness. As a young child, she talked too much in school and got in trouble frequently. Then, at the age of about eleven, she went "into lockdown." She became quiet and withdrawn. The spirited child went into the shadow, taking with it the natural, healthy narcissism that can say, "Hey! Look at me!" Selene has tearfully admitted that, though she is so happy that her daughter is a beautiful, confident young woman, she finds it bittersweet to see Katie having all the things she might have had but never did.

Selene has begun an effort to reconnect with this spirited self. In her outer life, she is experimenting with new relationships where her humor and vivacity are valued instead of discouraged. These new relationships are fraught with fear, however. When Selene allows herself to be assertive, to feel attractive, or to appreciate positive attention, the spoiling internalized voice of her mother interferes and threatens punishment for her audacity. Claiming these positive qualities that have been relegated to the shadow feels dangerous and illicit.

This was made clear when Selene brought in a dream that disturbed her greatly.

> *I say to my daughter that I am going to have sex with her.*
> *The door is opened by someone, and I am naked. We are rolling*
> *around but not feeling it. I can't do it. It's wrong. Katie is just*
> *going along with it, trying to make it work. She doesn't want to*
> *but won't say.*

I understood the dream to show symbolically that a part of Selene was seeking to integrate the shadow qualities her daughter carries that before had been dangerous and off-limits. The dream ego wants to have this intimate encounter with her daughter but then is unable to go through with it, because it seems so wrong. The incest theme was profoundly disturbing to Selene when she brought me the dream. She seemed only partially relieved when I shared with her my psychological understanding of it. The image of having intercourse with her daughter vividly expressed both her desire to claim the positive shadow qualities that her daughter carried and the degree to which claiming these qualities felt forbidden and dangerous. When our children live out positive potentials that we have had to disown, our relationship with them can feel emotionally charged.

Two weeks later, Selene had a second dream about Katie that seemed to validate our work on the first dream and to develop further the theme.

> *I am outside on a large grassy field, and long tables are set up*
> *on the grass in no particular order, but they are loaded with food.*
> *Each table seems to have a different kind of food—deli stuff,*
> *Mexican food, Greek food. I am milling around outside these*
> *tables that are ringed with people. I have an empty plate, and I*
> *want some of the food, but I can't get in. More accurately, no one*
> *offers to let me in, and I don't ask.*

> *I keep milling around the outside. Then, out of the sky, to*
> *the right of where I am, a bunch of young people drop onto a*
> *designated area with mats on the ground. I ask someone who*
> *they are, and I am told they are FBI trainees. Katie is one of*
> *the young people. We are all watching the "trainees" as they*
> *go through various physical exercises that demonstrate their*
> *amazing endurance and fitness. They do some other things and*
> *then they proceed to pass by us all as if they are in a graduation*
> *ceremony. Katie and the others pass me, looking ahead, sort of*
> *smiling, kind of like they are quietly proud. When they get by me,*
> *Katie turns around to look at me, and it is like I am looking at*
> *myself in the mirror. I am staring right into my own face. I am*
> *shocked and surprised, and I wake up.*

Selene described the FBI as an elite group, "the best of the best." She said that they often did bad things but in the interest of doing good. Her shadow daughter Katie is able to use her amazing fitness and endurance to accomplish things that are ultimately in the interest of wholeness and growth, even if this means behaving in a "bad" way. The dream ego, by contrast, is unable to harness enough assertive energy to claim any space at the table. But at the end of the dream, she recognizes herself in the strong, heroic figure of her daughter.

When our children carry positive shadow qualities for us, we have an opportunity to meet and accept those previously reviled aspects of ourselves that can renew and revivify us. The Norwegian fairy tale of "Tatterhood" beautifully illustrates the gifts of the positive shadow.

TATTERHOOD

Once upon a time, there was a king and queen who had no children, and that gave the queen much grief. At last, the king and queen took in a young girl to raise up as their own. One day, the girl was playing in the palace yard with a golden apple when a beggar woman and her child came by. Soon, the queen's ward and the beggar girl were playing together, tossing the apple between them.

The queen went to shoo away the beggar girl, but the child just stood there and said, "If you only knew my mother's power, you wouldn't send me away." When the queen asked what she meant, the girl told her how her mother could get her children if she chose. So the queen sent the girl to fetch her mother.

"Your daughter says that you can get me children," said the queen to the old woman as soon as she entered the room.

"One way to help you, perhaps I know," said the beggar wife. "Your Majesty must bring in two pails of water some evening before you go to bed. Wash in both of them and afterward throw the water under the bed. When you look under the bed the next morning, two flowers will have sprung up, one fair and one ugly. The fair one you must eat; the ugly one you must let stand. But mind you don't forget the last." That was what the beggar wife said.

The queen did just as the beggar wife had advised. She had the water brought up in two pails, washed in them, and emptied them under the bed. And lo, when she looked under the bed the next morning, there stood two flowers—one was ugly and foul, and had black leaves; the other was so bright, fair, and lovely, and she had never seen anything like it, so she ate it up at once. But the pretty flower tasted so sweet that she couldn't help herself. She ate the other up too, for she thought, *It can't hurt or help one much either way, I'll be bound.*

Well, sure enough, after a while, the queen was ready to give birth. First of all, she had a girl who had a wooden spoon in her hand and rode upon a goat. Loathly and ugly she was, and the very moment she came into the world she bawled out "Mamma!"

"If I'm your mamma," said the queen, "God give me grace to mend my ways."

"Oh, don't be sorry," said the girl, who rode on the goat, "for one will soon come after me who is better looking."

So, after a while, the queen had another girl, who was so fair and sweet, no one had ever set eyes on such a lovely child, and the queen was very pleased. The elder twin they called "Tatterhood," because she was always so ugly and ragged, and because she had a hood that hung about her ears in tatters. The queen could scarcely bear to look at her, and the nurses tried to shut her up in a room by herself, but it was all no good. Where the younger twin was, there she must also be, and no one could ever keep them apart.

Well, one Christmas eve, when they were half grown up, there rose such a frightful noise and clatter in the gallery outside the queen's bedroom. So Tatterhood asked what it was that dashed and crashed so out in the passage.

"Oh," said the queen, "it isn't worth asking about."

But Tatterhood wouldn't stop asking till she found out all about it, and so the queen told her it was a pack of trolls and witches who had come there to keep Christmas. So Tatterhood said she'd just go out and drive them away. She instructed the queen to mind and keep all the doors shut so that not one of them came so much as the least bit ajar. Having said this, off she went with her wooden spoon and began to hunt and sweep away the intruders. Now, somehow or other one door did get the least bit ajar, then her twin sister just peeped out to see how things were going with Tatterhood. But—*pop!*—up came an old witch who whipped off her head and stuck a calf's head on her shoulders instead. Then the princess ran back into the room on all fours and began to moo like a calf. When Tatterhood came back and saw her sister, she was very angry because they hadn't kept a better watch.

"But still, I'll see if I can't set her free," she said.

Then she asked the king for a ship in full trim and fully supplied, but explained she wouldn't need a captain or sailors. No, she would sail away with her sister all alone.

Then Tatterhood sailed to the land where the witches dwelled. She told her sister to stay on board and rode on her goat up to the witches' castle. When she got there, one of the windows in the gallery was open, and there she saw her sister's head hung up on the window frame. She leaped her goat through the window into the gallery, snapped up the head, and set off with it. The witches came after her, but Tatterhood beat and banged them with her wooden spoon, and so the pack of witches gave up. So Tatterhood got back to her ship, took the calf's head off her sister, and put her own on again, and then she became a girl as she had been before. After that, they sailed a long, long way, to a strange king's realm.

Now the king of that land was a widower and had an only son. When he saw the strange sail, he sent messengers down to find out who owned it. When the king's men came down there, they saw only Tatterhood, riding round and round the deck on her goat at full speed. They were amazed at this sight and asked if there were anyone else on board. "I have a sister," replied Tatterhood. "But no one shall see her other than the king himself."

When the king heard this strange story, he went at once to see the girl on the goat. When he arrived, Tatterhood led out her sister, and she was so fair and gentle that the king fell in love with her immediately. He brought them both back with him to the palace and wanted to have the sister for his queen, but Tatterhood said that the king could not marry her unless the king's son would marry Tatterhood. The prince was very reluctant to do this since Tatterhood was so ugly and wild, but at last, the king relented, though he was troubled to do so.

Soon the wedding day came. First, the king drove through town with his bride, and she was so lovely that all the people stopped to look at her. After then came the prince on horseback by the side of Tatterhood, who trotted along on her goat with her wooden spoon in her fist. To look at him, it was more like going to a burial than a wedding. He was sad and didn't speak.

"Why don't you talk?" asked Tatterhood when they had ridden a bit.

"Why, what should I talk about?" answered the prince.

"Well, you might at least ask me why I ride upon this ugly goat," said Tatterhood.

"Why do you ride on that ugly goat?" asked the Prince.

"Is it an ugly goat? Why it's the grandest horse a bride ever rode on," answered Tatterhood. And just like that, the goat became a horse—the finest the prince had ever seen.

Then they rode on again a bit, but the prince was just as woeful as before and didn't speak. So Tatterhood asked him again why he didn't talk, and when the prince answered that he didn't know what to talk about, she said, "You can at least ask me why I ride with this ugly spoon in my fist."

"Why do you ride with that ugly spoon?" asked the prince.

"Is it an ugly spoon? Why it's the loveliest silver wand a bride ever bore," said Tatterhood, and just like that, it became a silver wand, so dazzlingly bright that the sunbeams glistened from it.

So they rode on another bit, but the prince was just as sorrowful and never said a word. In a little while, Tatterhood asked him again why he didn't talk and bade him ask why she wore that ugly gray hood on her head.

"Why do you wear that ugly gray hood on your head?" asked the prince.

"Is it an ugly hood? Why it's the brightest golden crown a bride ever wore," answered Tatterhood, and it became a crown on the spot.

They rode on for a long while, and the prince was still sorrowful and silent. So his bride asked him again why he didn't talk and bade him ask now why her face was so ugly.

"Ah!" asked the prince, "why is your face so ugly?"

"I ugly?" said Tatterhood. "You think my sister pretty, but I am ten times prettier," and when the prince looked at her, she was so lovely that he thought there never was so lovely a woman in all the world.

So they drank the bridal cup both deep and long, and, if you make haste and run to the king's palace, I dare say you'll find there's still a drop of the bridal ale left for you.

The tale begins with a childless royal couple. The ruling principle is a sterile one, from which no new life can come. The twins in the story are foreshadowed and doubled by the stranger lassie and her beggar friend. Although the stranger lassie plays with a golden apple—a symbol, perhaps, of fertility, immortality, or wholeness—there is no change to the status quo until the beggar girl enters the tale, and the two girls toss the apple between them.

COMMITMENT TO GROWTH

Doubling in fairy tales or dreams can refer to something that is getting closer to conscious integration. In this story, there are two sets of twin girls. The queen in the tale indeed seems to be struggling mightily with bringing something to fruition. She adopts the "stranger lassie" so that she can have the experience of motherhood, and when she hears that the beggar woman can help her become pregnant, she overcomes the dictates of propriety to speak with her.

I have seen this unswerving commitment and resultant willingness to overstep collective conventions with patients or friends who have difficulty conceiving, and in response, become totally committed to doing whatever it takes to become a mother. Many women who have trouble getting pregnant will go to heroic lengths—assisted fertility or adoption—to have the desired child. While their single-minded drive sometimes invites judgment on the part of friends or society, they are following an inner injunction with passion and commitment.

So, too, some patients exhibit this same degree of single-minded commitment to their individuation journey. They faithfully record their dreams and come in week after week even though the work is difficult and often painful. The queen wants a child and will defy convention to have one. Already, we see that this queen has the potential to be open to the dark side. She is not so bound up in her queenly persona that she won't talk to the beggar woman.

As in the West African fairy tale explored in the previous chapter, the adoption of a child precedes a pregnancy. This appears to be the case frequently in actuality, as the following quote from a medical journal points out.

> There would seem to be a longstanding belief, bordering
> on myth, that adoption or even the decision to adopt
> increases conceptive capacity in infertile women. A number
> of infertile women state that they intend to adopt in order
> that they might conceive. The author has even been consulted
> professionally by a patient who considered that her period of
> infertility was ended when her pet dog had a litter of puppies![1]

Adopt comes from the Latin word that means "to choose for oneself." To adopt is to make a very serious, even sacred commitment to something. Actual adoptions are permanent and binding. Adoption differs significantly from conception in that it must be consciously chosen.

A woman can, of course, conceive without intending or even wanting to be a mother. The adoptive mother, on the other hand, usually has had to work at having a child.

The queen's adoption of the beggar brat means that there are two sets of "twin" girls in the story. The doubling of the motif of twin girls also serves to emphasize that it is not possible to have one without the other. Where there is brightness and beauty, shadow will be constellated. The darkness is needed to balance the light. And as the tale eloquently points out, it is in the fertile opposition between brightness and shadow that something new can arise. The stranger lassie and the tattered beggar's brat tossing a gold apple between them is an image of the dynamic holding of the tension of opposites. It is when the queen sees this that she taps on the window and asks the children to come to her. Through this action, the sterility of the ruling couple ends.

RENEWAL COMES FROM DARKNESS

What has been disowned by the conscious personality and cast into the shadow often holds the key to renewal. Here, it is the beggar woman who knows the secret to generativity. The queen must wash in two pails of water and then cast the dirty water under the bed. Once again, the tale emphasizes that new life springs from that which we have rejected—in this case, the water that we have used to cleanse the filth from our bodies.

The bed is associated with nighttime, sexuality, and unconsciousness. Under the bed is often a dark and dusty place where things are hidden or stored away. Again, the queen is confronted with a shadow element in the form of an ugly flower. As with the beggar girl and her mother, the queen shows ambivalence, reacting initially with disgust or disapproval but then showing herself to be open to what the shadow side might have to offer. She doesn't hesitate long before welcoming in the shadow by consuming the black flower. When we as mothers are open to the shadowy side of life, we find that renewal and new potentials can arise in unexpected places.

The theme of turning to the shadow side to nurture renewal and new life is a common one in fairy tales. In "Biancabella and the Snake," conception does not happen until the snake enters the queen's womb. When Rapunzel's mother becomes pregnant with a much-longed-for child, she is drawn into a dark pact with the witch in whose garden grows the life-sustaining herb. The German fairy tale "The Black Princess" also begins with a childless king and queen.

> The queen desperately wants to have a child, but they had none. A river runs through the town, with a bridge spanning it. On the right side of the bridge is a crucifix; on the left side, a stone figure of Lucifer.... The queen goes regularly to the bridge and cries and prays to Christ to give her a child, but after a while she becomes tired of doing this and getting no results, so she decides to turn to the devil. Then, after three months, she finds herself pregnant.[2]

In this tale, new life also comes from the dark side, but here the split between the opposites is far more extreme. The shadow is further from consciousness, and its character is more archetypal, as it is carried by Lucifer rather than a beggar woman. As we might expect, the redemption of the shadow is more difficult and bloodier in "The Black Princess" than it is in our Norwegian tale.

The following dream of a woman eight weeks pregnant illustrates the generative function of the shadow.

> *I am on the lower level of the subway system. A young black woman gives me a diamond. I put it deep into my pocket, not wanting people to know for fear they will steal it. When I reach the upper level, I feel safer.*[3]

The dreamer connected the diamond with her pregnancy. It is not unusual for Caucasian Americans to have dreams where something valuable but not previously recognized as such is associated with a dream figure who is African American. In the United States, African Americans have long held our cultural shadow, often serving as the scapegoats for white culture. This dreamer receives a precious treasure from a shadowy woman in a dark, subterranean realm. Psychologically, new life cannot come from the conscious side of the personality alone. This is a lesson that we will learn as we mother.

If you have been accustomed to living according to the dictates of the collective, becoming a mother will require a new attitude, an openness to those parts of yourself that may not before have been valued. In a genuine way, the current increase in fertility issues among women has at least something to do with a one-sided attitude toward what in our culture is typically in the shadow. When a woman chooses to delay childbirth to pursue a career or educational goals, she may be taking her fertility for granted, assuming it will be there when wanted. In many contexts, it would be considered embarrassingly unsophisticated for a woman to admit that she might want children. Psychologist and author Daphne de Marneffe writes that *motherhood* and *desire* conventionally don't belong in the same sentence in our culture.[4] To admit that we long for a child, as the queen does in our fairy tale, is to lose some of our ego's hubris and open ourselves up to the undervalued wisdom of the instincts. Moreover, just as the queen humbles herself by putting herself in the hands of the beggar woman, when we admit our longing to be pregnant, our ego is humbled because we have acknowledged a passionate desire for something that is out of conscious control. We must entrust ourselves to our body's unknowable workings.

Memoirist Kathryn Lynard Soper describes how she experienced her own "baby hunger" as welling up from some deep place within her, in a way that contradicted her ego-driven expectations of how she would move forward in the world of success and academic achievement.

When Reed and I were engaged, we talked about having a few children years down the road, after I earned the Ph.D. I dreamed about—maybe by then I'd actually want to be a mother.

But that was before I met a newborn baby for the first time.

After our wedding, Reed and I lived in a basement apartment near Brigham Young University, next door to our friends Luis and Eva. They brought their firstborn home one morning in the dry burn of August. When Eva opened the door to my knock, her eyes were shadowed, her hair limp, her curves sagging. But she smiled, quick and sure, as she glanced backward over her shoulder. Behind her I saw a pink blanket smoothed over the worn brown carpet, and on the blanket, an infant asleep. My legs moved forward as my eyes took in the sight: flesh and blood and bone, impossibly small, impossibly alive.

I sat at the edge of the blanket. Eva followed, gingerly, still sore from the birth. Time slowed as we watched the gentle rise and fall of the baby's chest, the short jerks of her limbs as she startled in her sleep. Dressed lightly for the summer heat, her pink skin glowed with a sheen that filled the room, washing the dullness from the worn furniture and yellowed linoleum and dark-paneled doors. The light touched me and sent me spinning. . . .

Six months after my wedding, I told my senior advisor that I didn't need her letter of recommendation after all. I wasn't going to graduate school—I was going to have a baby. She shook her head, disappointed that I was succumbing to "cultural pressure," the Mormon expectation for young married couples to bear children as quickly as possible. She was wrong. My unexpected longing for a child didn't come from anything or anyone external. It was a deep, true desire that came from the deepest, truest part of myself, and I trusted it completely.[5]

Soper's first experience of a newborn is deeply numinous. Focused as she was on academic achievement, her desire for children had been in the shadow.

SHADOW CHILD

As the tale continues, Tatterhood shows immediate recognition of the queen when she bawls out "Mamma!" The queen doesn't recognize Tatterhood as one of her own, yet Tatterhood knows the queen to be her mother. When some shadow content becomes conscious for the first time, it may appear alien and even grotesque to us, and we may be reluctant to acknowledge the family resemblance. When this shadow quality is carried by our child, it is harder for us to disown it because we cannot deny the child is ours. This can be uncomfortable, as it is then more difficult to defend against knowing this about ourselves by splitting it off. We may be forced to consider that these objectionable qualities are not necessarily "other."

When we have more than one child, there is the ever-present psychic temptation to split—to assign certain projected qualities to one child and certain others to another child. In extreme cases, this can look like our fairy tale, where there is a light child and a shadow child. British psychoanalyst Rozsika Parker details such a story about a woman named Maeve with twin daughters in her book *Torn in Two*. "When her daughters were born," Parker writes, "Maeve looked at Cathy and thought to herself, *Here is a member of my family*, but her daughter Coral appeared 'like a complete alien.'"[6] Like the queen in "Tatterhood," the experience of projecting shadow onto one of the twins happened spontaneously, at the moment of their birth. Maeve's girls were ten when the interview from which the following is excerpted took place.

> I feel I can communicate with Cathy in a way that seems
> impossible with Coral. She and I very quickly get into a
> position of deep hostility. Sometimes I feel she needs me
> there in order to have what can feel [*sic*] a rather abusive
> relationship. I feel abused by her. I always have done. As a
> baby if you changed her nappy before she had had her feed,
> she just got full of rage. Things had to be done in the order
> in which she wished them to be.[7]

It is easy to hear in this quote Maeve's projections onto her daughter. She ascribes adult emotions and reactions to her child, even as an infant. Parker goes on to report that Maeve finds in Cathy many of the characteristics she most values in herself. Cathy also tends to get depressed, as does Maeve.

> Maeve describes Coral as imperious and thoughtless—
> aspects of herself that she passionately does not want to
> acknowledge. It is as if a hateful bundle of repudiated
> qualities is being handed down. . . . She locates everything
> in herself of vulnerable value in Cathy and everything
> relating to unacceptable rage and rapaciousness in Coral.
> She recognizes that she and Coral share a capacity for rage.
> . . . Despite her insight, Maeve has a sense of being drawn
> helplessly into conflict against her better judgement.[8]

As with our fairy tale, the fair daughter is associated with desirable qualities, but she is also vulnerable and weak and needs protection. Coral, on the other hand, is associated with many objectionable qualities but is strong and resourceful. Like Tatterhood, Coral is also fearless.

> When Cathy was learning to read, she would never
> read anything with a giant or witch in it. She couldn't, for
> example, even open a book with Little Red Riding Hood in
> it. I bought her a lovely version of *The Water Babies* but she
> found it too scary, and so I gave it to Coral. She loves it. She
> can go to the most terrifying films without turning a hair.
> Wicked witches hold no horror for her—they never have.[9]

Perhaps Coral doesn't need to fear wicked witches because she, like Tatterhood, has an affinity with them since she is the shadow child. Coral bravely takes on things that may have frightened her mother, and in so doing, lives out Maeve's unlived life in a positive way. If Maeve could let Coral be her guide in this respect, she might come into a conscious relationship with her imperiousness, thoughtlessness, rage, rapaciousness, and fearlessness, and to see these qualities as potentially positive. If she were able to lay claim to some of that energy that she found so objectionable, she might discover that she needn't get depressed as much.

As Tatterhood and her sister grow, the queen reacts with ambivalence to this shadow element. She can barely stand to look at her and tries to shut her away. In psychological language, it is difficult to see our shadows, and we would like to hide away those parts of ourselves that have been deemed unacceptable. And yet this is not possible. You cannot have one side without the other, and so too for Tatterhood and her fair sister. Where one twin was, there was the other also, and no one could separate them.

As it turns out, the queen is fortunate to have such a wild and lively shadow child. When the witches come, the queen not only doesn't know what to do about the situation but needs to deny what is happening. But Tatterhood doesn't let her mother remain in denial. She forces the story out of her, and she knows what needs to be done. Jungian analyst Murray Stein likens the shadow to a country's "secret espionage system" that operates "without the explicit knowledge of the head of state, who is therefore allowed to deny culpability."[10] (This is similar to Selene's associations to the FBI in the dream discussed earlier in this chapter.) So Tatterhood does the stately queen's "dirty work," riding forth to chase the witches away. Often, it is our shadow side that best knows how to react to a difficult situation. It is as if the shadow stands behind us, waiting until the conscious personality faces a dire challenge, and it is needed. It takes the shadow to know how to deal with the shadowy things. The wild, untamed side of our personality has access to the instinctual knowledge that is needed in a crisis. It is witches that Tatterhood has to fight off, and we know already from the fact that she rides a goat that she has an affiliation with this underworld feminine shadow element. In the Middle Ages, witches were known to ride on goats.

GROWING MORE WHOLE

Marnie was a mother in my practice who was also helped by her "shadow child." A highly successful attorney who had always been oriented to achievement, Marnie had high expectations for her son right from the beginning. But he wouldn't comply. "He was never the kind of kid you could rush," Marnie mused. "And he never cared about winning." At first, Marnie found this difficult at times. She had envisioned her child being a star athlete and student. But Ryan always seemed to dance to the beat of his own drum. "He was wonderfully quirky! He would have long, hilarious conversations with his feet when we rode in the car," Marnie recalls. As he grew older, Ryan became interested in theater rather than athletics. His perfect comedic timing made him a star performer at his high school. Marnie feels that Ryan has been an important teacher for her, helping her to reconnect with her silliness and creativity that were not valued in her family of origin.

In the final section of the tale, Tatterhood tells the king he cannot have her sister as a wife unless the prince takes her to wife also. The shadow side is asking for acceptance and acknowledgment. When the shadow is accepted and acknowledged, it can be seen for what it really is—"90 percent pure gold," according to Jung.[11] Asking the right questions facilitates transformation. When we approach our unloved selves with curiosity rather than judgment, we value those parts of ourselves for perhaps the first time. Projections fall away, and what before appeared shameful and lowly can be seen for its true worth.

The tale ends with a double wedding, an image of the successful completion of the process of transformation. When the positive shadow holds for us essential parts of ourselves with which we had long ago lost conscious contact, then getting to know our shadow can lead us to an encounter with the guiding self. We grow more whole and come closer to living out our unique, individual destiny. Opening ourselves to these repudiated qualities may be painful, but it will also result in our consciousness being fundamentally changed. We may find ourselves questioning things that we had long taken for granted, such as our values, preferences, and strengths. Instead of living the falsehoods we created for ourselves in the process of adapting to parental and cultural expectations, we begin living our truth that we somehow lost touch with along the way.

Questions for Reflection
for Valuing Darkness

1. The queen in the story longs for a child. She is so committed to this goal that she is willing to do some unqueenly things, such as eat the black flower. Have you ever wanted something

so badly that you were willing to do things that were uncharacteristic of you to get them? What happened as a result?

2. When Tatterhood is born, the queen is horrified and wants to hide her away. When have you felt this way about one of your children? About aspects of yourself? What parts of your personality do you feel ashamed of and would like to hide?

3. When the witches come to the castle, Tatterhood is the person who knows how to deal with this. In what areas may your child know how to handle things better than you do? What qualities does that child live out that you may be cut off from?

4. If we have more than one child, it may be the case that one is more like us, while another carries qualities that we may have disowned in ourselves. Do you find that you relate more easily to one child than another? Is one of your children a "shadow child?" If so, what has he or she taught you about yourself?

5. Tatterhood is seen as ugly, odd, and undesirable. Where have you felt like this in your life? What is it like to feel this way, and what have you done about it?

6. At the end of the tale, we learn that Tatterhood's true nature shines through if asked the right question. If we approach shadow qualities with the right attitude, we will often see their enormous value. When recently have you come to appreciate a quality in either yourself or your child that you once considered to be predominantly negative?

7. What behaviors or traits in your children trigger emotions of disgust, shame, or disapproval? Are you able to see that these qualities might be valuable in some contexts?

CHAPTER 6

Embodying Darkness

The greatest advantage of not having children must be
that you can go on believing that you are a nice person:
once you have children, you realize how wars start.

FAY WELDON
IN TORN IN TWO

t wasn't the first time that I had ever gotten angry at my daughter, but it was the first time some line had been crossed, something had been irrevocably broken. For the first two years of her life, I had responded to her needs with mostly endless patience and warmth. Though there had been times when I was tested, I could generally think of myself as a good mother.

But one day that changed. I was tired, having not been able to sleep well for weeks on end due to being eight months pregnant. My daughter was sleeping through the night, but just barely. I would sleep fitfully, wake up to racing, anxious thoughts in the middle of the night, fall back asleep around 3 or 4 a.m., only to have my daughter wake up for the day at 5:30 a.m. Each morning I woke up more tired than the day before. Mothers at my playgroup would often ruefully remind one another that under the Geneva Conventions, sleep deprivation is defined as torture.

On this morning, I lumbered downstairs and started making breakfast. My daughter, fresh and energetic, sat happily on the floor, paging through a book and chattering nonsensically as she "read" it to herself. Dizzy with exhaustion, I made the coffee and oatmeal in slow motion.

I strapped her into her high chair. She noticed a spider on the window and asked me about it.

"Why siber inside?" she wanted to know. Her question interrupted my internal debate about whether I should run errands that day.

"I guess he thought he might like it in here," I said, too tired to come up with a better (more playful? more informative? more creative?) answer.

"Why?" she asked. A glob of oatmeal slid down the front of her pajamas and embedded itself irretrievably in the high chair's frame. *Should I risk driving?* I wondered to myself. I had read that severe sleep deprivation was at least as impairing to drivers as alcohol intoxication. *Did I have the energy to face the megastore with my toddler?*

"Maybe there is more food for him inside, or he doesn't like the rain," I replied.

"Why?" she asked again. And yet it was almost more difficult being at home with her. At least if we got out, there were distractions for us both. At home, there were piles of laundry, a present for a niece that had to be ordered, calls that had to be made. In the end, I decided not to go, but I was full of doubt as to whether I had made the right decision. In my exhaustion, this had become a monumental decision without a right answer.

"I don't know, honey, okay? Maybe he just likes it better," I said, my tone getting edgy.

"Why?" she questioned.

I sighed and collected the dishes. There was oatmeal on the floor now too. My thoughts found their way to their habitual groove of worry, guilt, and self-doubt. *How will I manage when the new baby comes?* I thought. My daughter screamed and squirmed as I wiped oatmeal off her face, hands, and clothes, more roughly, perhaps, than I should have. I was only partially successful, of course, which meant that there would be pieces of oatmeal on the couch later. *If I switched the babysitter to Tuesday afternoons only,* I thought, *and saw more clients on the weekend, then maybe my practice wouldn't be affected as much.* I thought about such changes to my work and babysitting schedules obsessively, hoping that somehow, I could make everything fit and make sense. I would need more childcare to continue my practice and training, but I already felt bad about the time the sitter was coming. And leaving the newborn with the sitter was going to feel even worse.

I sat on the couch, vaguely aware that the rug beneath the clutter of toys and books badly needed vacuuming. My daughter brought me one of her dolls and shoved it toward me. "Pay with me!" she commanded. I half-heartedly made the doll walk along the coffee table and go to the kitchen of his little house, but she soon became frustrated with my efforts and began imperiously directing me to make the doll climb up on the roof, for what reason I could not imagine.

I was lonely for adult company. It would have been nice to take a walk with a neighbor who also had a little girl. But, seemingly like all the rest of the world, she worked, and her daughter was in day care. Would day care be a better option? But I didn't like that idea. I turned on the TV to give myself a break. My daughter sat rapt before it. My neighbor's daughter, who was in day care, was at that moment probably engaging in a stimulating finger rhyme, not watching *Jay Jay the Jet Plane*. More guilt. More fear. More self-doubt. These emotions mixed with exhaustion to create a toxic, potent brew—an oily concoction of anxiety, self-doubt, and simmering resentment that was slowly working itself into explosive rage.

"Okay, baby girl!" I said as the show ended, attempting to sound both cheerful and authoritative. "Time to turn off the TV." I flicked off the set and closed the door to the small TV cabinet. Predictably, she began screaming, fiercely waving her hands in the air and grabbing on the cabinet so that I was afraid she would pull it over on herself. "Do you want to go outside?" I said, pulling her away from the tottering TV. I didn't have the energy to come up with a creative distraction. The tantrum was getting worse. Her face was red, her mouth screwed up. She was wailing. It was only 8 a.m., but for both of us, it had already been a long morning. In her frustration, she reached for a piece of paper on the coffee table and began ripping it. The exterminator contract. It had taken me weeks to take care of that. We would need that when we sold the house. I was angry at myself for having left it on the coffee table, but I was no longer capable of that degree of discernment. My rage poured forth.

"Don't you dare do that!" I snarled. The release felt *good*! Her little face registered fear, and some part of me saw that and winced, but the stream of molten anger would not be staunched now that it had been loosed. I bent down, putting my face close to hers. "How dare you! Don't you do that!" I was at full volume, my face contorted with irrational fury. She drew back in terror and confusion, crying. She was so distraught that she vomited.

In the moments that followed, all the anger was gone and just sadness remained. I cried and held her, apologizing to her. I remember thinking, *Today is the day I learned that I am not a good mother.* I had seen my own shadow.

SEEING OUR SHADOW

Motherhood may offer us one of the few places in our lives where we can see most clearly our own shadow because it pushes us to such extreme feeling states. Whether you are provoked by a self-sabotaging teen who can't ever seem to hand in assignments on time or a school-aged child whose inability to make friends dismays you, you will likely be caught off guard by the ferocity of your negative feelings toward your child. Inevitably, our children will provoke our shadow side. Most parents who are honest about it will admit to being shocked at their capacity for rage, hatred, and cruelty toward their children. Never before having children did I ever experience the primal, uncontrolled rage that I have felt at times since.

The energies in the deep interior are very different from the part of ourselves we consciously present to the world. Some of what we encounter during our sojourn at the bottom of the well will be truly frightening and alien. It may be a struggle not to be overtaken by powerful emotions we didn't know we were capable of feeling. Through the experience of mothering, we will doubtless have many occasions when we project subtler aspects of our shadows on our children, as discussed in previous chapters. We will also likely have moments where our personas are ripped away by a flood of primitive emotion, and we are possessed by shadow. When this happens to us, it is difficult not to have the utterly humbling experience of knowing ourselves at our very worst.

As Fay Weldon's quote at the start of the chapter implies, motherhood will invariably introduce us to the less familiar, deeper strata of our humanity, where we are capable of the most destructive and reprehensible of acts. To understand how wars start, we must be aware of our capacity for violence and destruction. At an intellectual level, we may be aware that we are hypothetically capable of terrible things just by virtue of being human, but we may never before have met those parts of ourselves. In response to the news that Andrea Yates had drowned her five children in the bathtub in 2001, columnist Anna Quindlen wrote an opinion piece in *Newsweek* that sparked great interest and discussion. In "Playing God on No Sleep," Quindlen acknowledges that most women can relate at some level to Yates's murderous feelings.

> Every mother I've asked about the Yates case has the
> same reaction. She's appalled; she's aghast. And then
> she gets this look. And the look says that at some
> forbidden level, she understands. The look says that
> there are two very different kinds of horror here: there
> is the unimaginable idea of the killings, and then there
> is the entirely imaginable idea of going quietly bonkers
> in the house with five kids under the age of seven.[1]

Even though most of us would never act on our murderous feelings toward our children, most of us will admit in our more honest moments that we can at least imagine *having* those feelings, if only momentarily. Motherhood will likely expose us to deep layers of the unconscious inside all of us, wherein resides what we might call "evil."

In the Hindu pantheon, the goddess Kali is both the benevolent good mother and the destructive terrible mother. In her beneficent form, she is life-giving and nurturing. In her right hand, she holds a beautiful, bejeweled golden ladle. In her left hand, she carries a vessel of abundance that she uses to give all her children sweet rice milk. For the vast majority of us, it will be easy to identify consciously with this energy and the feelings it brings up. However, there will be other times when we will feel frightened by the depth of our rage, hatred, or coldness toward our child. At these times, we will be experiencing the archetypal energy of the terrible mother.

In her destructive aspect, Kali appears as an emaciated, gruesome hag, who wears a necklace of human skulls and feasts voraciously on the entrails of her victims. We may not have known before having children that we had Kali's darker side within us as well. I remember being asked before I had children if I could identify with sadistic feelings. I honestly couldn't find that within myself at the time. But a part of me *did* enjoy raging at my daughter that day, even if just for a moment. When we find ourselves experiencing this kind of energy, for most of us it can feel as though we have been taken over by a force outside ourselves. We would like very much to deny that those feelings are a part of us.

Shadowy, primitive emotions such as rage can be problematic, even destructive. They may pose moral concerns, especially as regards their manifestations around our children. But if we banish Kali to our psychic underworld, then we both lose access to her vivifying energy and risk being possessed by her because we do not have a conscious relationship with her. And yet there is no question that she is one dangerous lady. Certainly we ought not to let her roam free through our psychic landscape. How should we relate to this energy? And how can we integrate and own it?

The Irish fairy tale "The Horned Women" can perhaps guide us in thinking about how we might best relate to this dark, archetypal shadow energy. It tells the tales of one mother's encounter with this frightening force.

THE HORNED WOMEN

A rich woman sat up late one night carding and preparing wool while all the family and servants were asleep. Suddenly a knock was given at the door, and a voice called, "Open! Open!"

"Who is there?" said the woman of the house.

"I am the Witch of One Horn" came the answer.

The mistress opened the door, and a woman with one horn on her forehead entered, carrying wool carders with her. She sat down by the fire in silence and began to card the wool with violent haste. Suddenly she paused, and said aloud, "Where are the women? They delay too long."

Then a second knock came to the door, and a voice called as before, "Open! Open!" The mistress felt obliged to rise and open to the call, and immediately a second witch entered, having two horns on her forehead, and in her hand a wheel for spinning wool. "I am the Witch of the Two Horns," she said, and she began to spin as quick as lightning.

And so the knocks went on, and the witches entered, until at last twelve women sat round the fire—the first with one horn, the last with twelve horns.

They carded and spun and wove, singing an ancient rhyme, but they didn't speak. The mistress of the house was frozen with terror. She tried to call for help, but she couldn't move or speak because she was under the witches' spell.

Then one of them said to her, "Rise, woman, and make us a cake." The mistress searched for a vessel to bring water from the well that she might mix the meal and make the cake, but she could find none.

And they said to her, "Take a sieve and bring water in it." She took the sieve and went to the well, but the water poured from it, so she sat down by the well and wept. Then a voice spoke and said, "Take yellow clay and moss and bind them together, then plaster the sieve so that it will hold." This she did, and the sieve held the water for the cake.

Then the voice said, "Return to your house and cry aloud three times, 'The mountain of the Fenian women and the sky over it are all on fire.'" And she did so.

When the witches inside heard the call, a terrible cry broke from their lips. They rushed forth with wild shrieks and fled back to their home. The Spirit of the Well then instructed the mistress on how to protect her house against the witches if they ever returned.

And first, she sprinkled the water in which she had washed her children's feet on the threshold. Next, she took the cake that, in her absence, the witches had made of meal mixed with the blood drawn from the sleeping family. She broke the cake in bits and placed a bit in the mouth of each sleeper. When her sleeping children tasted the cake, they were restored. Then she took the cloth the witches had woven and placed it half in and half out of the chest. Lastly, she secured the door with a great crossbeam fastened in the jambs so that the witches could not enter. Having done these things, she waited.

It wasn't long before the witches returned. They raged and called for vengeance and demanded that the door be opened to them, but the preparations the mistress had taken held fast against their enchantments. Then the witches rushed away filled with fury, but the woman and the house were left in peace, and a mantle dropped by one of the witches in her flight was kept hung up by the mistress in memory of that night, and this mantle was kept by the same family from generation to generation for five hundred years after.

These witches who spin and card with "violent haste" take possession of the woman's home in the middle of the night while she is engaged in a solitary activity. When we are alone, we are more susceptible to eruptions from the unconscious. Many mothers spend all day working outside the home, care for their children in the evenings, and then find themselves folding laundry or completing office work after everyone goes to sleep. What might this woman be feeling as she sits up late, tired and hoping for sleep but continuing to work long after everyone else is in bed? One can imagine her at her task, thinking about her situation and its unfairness, feeling the resentfulness build up with each pass of the cards, one over the other, until it gives rise to a knock at the door—the entry of dark, primitive emotionality, possibly including rage. The day I became enraged at my daughter was the first time the witches knocked on my door.

When we get this angry, it can be as if our ego is under a spell, and though we may be watching ourselves do things we know we shouldn't, we are powerless to stop ourselves. We have the humbling experience of knowing our conscious self is not in charge. We see how divided our psyche is. One part very much doesn't want to do what we are doing. Another part is enjoying it.

RAGE

In my experience, as both a friend and a therapist to other mothers, I am struck by the absence of specific discussions of rage. Judging from conversations I have had with other mothers, I would believe that I am the only one to have lost control in this way. (By the way, I am chagrined to admit that that was hardly the last time.) Mothers will admit to being angry, of course. But they rarely talk about specifics. Perhaps incidents such as the one I describe are unusual, but I suspect not.

Some writers have had the courage to share their rages. Interestingly, these accounts are most often softened by humor, as if maternal rage is so dangerous, fearful, or threatening that it cannot be held without a dose of normalizing laughter. I found a few personal stories, however, that did not resort to humor. In "Crossing the Line in the Sand: How Mad Can Mother Get?" Elissa Schappell writes of a night trying to put her two kids to bed after a long and stressful day of juggling her career and her parenting responsibilities. Her son Miles has just thrown a book that hit her on the brow bone and is watching her, amused, to see what she'll do next.

> My blood, spiked with stress, rage, and guilt, surges in
> my veins, and I feel almost dizzy. In a fury, I jump up on the
> ladder and make to grab Miles around the throat. He and
> Isadora skitter backward, bolting to the wall to get out of my
> reach. Now they know: I can see it in their faces. I am going
> to take Miles down, or better, take them both down, and I
> can't wait. I want to hurt him. An otherworldly bellow of hell
> and doom swells in my gut, and a terrible sound rises out of
> me, as though this ugliness has been boiling in my bowels for
> years. I roar at them.
>
> In slow motion, I watch my children's faces draw into masks
> of fear and shock. Miles yelps. Isadora presses her face into the
> crook of her arm. "I'm scared!" she cries, her voice breaking.
>
> "Good!" I scream, meaning it. "I'm *glad* you're scared! You
> *should* be scared!"

But I am scared, too—scared of hurting my children, of not being able to protect them from myself. Scared of how much I both love them and hate them in this moment. . . .

"Mommy," Isadora whimpers, her face wet with tears. "Please stop. Please. You're scaring us."

Mommy, please stop! My daughter's pleading is like taking a knife to an elevator cable, snap! And my rage goes into free fall, leaving this great emptiness, this hollow ring of silence . . .[2]

When we are seized by these dark, archetypal energies, it can very much feel as though we, too, are being devoured by them. It is frightening to realize the depth of rage of which we are capable and to feel momentarily possessed by this monstrous energy over which we seemingly have little control.

Schappell's rage is brought to an abrupt end by her daughter's pleading, just as my fury was cut short by my daughter's distress. There is a story about the goddess Kali that illuminates this experience. Kali has been ordered to kill a demon. She has severed his head and is dancing around the battlefield with it, but she cannot be calmed and is in danger of destroying the universe in her anger. When Shiva is called upon to rein in Kali's fury, he transforms himself into a crying baby and puts himself in her path. This awakens Kali's motherly nature and she goes to comfort the crying child, all of her rage evaporating in an instant. As mothers, we can be called back from rage when our instinct to care for and comfort our child is evoked.

As with the personal stories recounted above, the forces in the fairy tale are destructive to the children in the house. The witches are draining the children's blood to make their cake. This energy needs to be dealt with appropriately, lest it destroy us or those close to us.

BENEFITS OF ANGER

Yet these witches undoubtedly have a positive aspect as well. The symbolism associated with them lets us know they are powerful divinities. They are spinners and weavers, and as we have seen before, these are powerful metaphors. Spinning is associated with bringing forth and fostering life. Spinning and weaving are aspects of the goddess who, like Kali, both creates and destroys. In her destructive aspect, she is the one who cuts the thread of fate. Horns are associated with divine power, aggression, strength, and protectiveness. These are goddesses of great creative significance. We would cut ourselves off from their power only at great cost to ourselves.

Sometimes what is needed in parenting is hot and fierce, rather than soft and tender. As in the case of the princess who hurls the frog against the wall and finds that this violent act—full of embodied authenticity, as anger often is—has transformed the lowly creature into a prince, it may be passion rather than compassion that is needed to break the spell and restore relatedness. It is possible to connect with our children at times through hate and anger rather than through love. Hate and anger may also sometimes be what is needed for us to feel connected with ourselves.

When our shadowy feelings of rage make an appearance, we will be more authentic than when we repress these feelings. In the end, authenticity is required for genuine relatedness, whether that relatedness is to our children or ourselves. Our anger matters because it is authentic.

Anger can help you find your true stance. It can give you the fire you need to stand firm and set limits—with your children and with others. And being angry with our kids also teaches them how to be angry. When my daughter was four, I befriended Beth, who also had a four-year-old daughter named Mindi. Beth was a very thoughtful and intelligent person who herself had been subjected to much abusive treatment as a child. She confided in me that she had felt very damaged by this, and she had sworn when she became pregnant that she would never speak harshly to her child. She told me about the tremendous self-restraint she had cultivated in order to keep this promise to herself.

One day, my daughter and I were visiting Beth and Mindi at their home. While my daughter and Mindi were playing, Beth went upstairs for a moment. With her mother out of sight, Mindi pushed my daughter, knocking her down. I witnessed the incident quite clearly. Mindi's aggression was entirely unprovoked, as far as I could tell. My daughter began crying. "It's not okay to push someone, Mindi," I said, while tending to my daughter. At that moment, Beth returned. "Mindi doesn't push," she answered me, matter-of-factly. I was quite flummoxed and wasn't sure what to say.

It was clear that Beth genuinely believed that her daughter was incapable of aggression. It was as if she had so effectively cut herself off from her own aggression that she could not imagine it to exist in her child. Anger had been so effectively banished from consciousness in this family that it was free to roam unchecked in the unconscious, behind Mom's back, as it were. It struck me that Mindi was not being helped by having her aggressiveness erased so completely. She never got to see her mother angry and therefore never learned that anger can be normal and healthy, or that people can survive being angry at one another.

The incident with Beth and Mindi recalled for me a Grimm's fairy tale about a "too good mother."

SWEET PORRIDGE

There was a poor but good little girl who lived alone with her mother, and they no longer had anything to eat. So the child went into the forest, and there an aged woman met her who was aware of her sorrow, and presented her with a little pot, which when she said, "Cook, little pot, cook," would cook good, sweet porridge, and when she said, "Stop, little pot," it ceased to cook. The girl took the pot home to her mother, and now they were freed from their poverty and hunger, and they ate sweet porridge as often as they chose. Once, when the girl had gone out, her mother said, "Cook, little pot, cook." And it cooked, and she ate till she was satisfied, and then she wanted the pot to stop cooking but did not know the word. So it went on cooking, and the porridge rose over the edge, and still it cooked on until the kitchen and whole house were full, and then the next house, and then the whole street, just as if it wanted to satisfy the hunger of the whole world. And there was the greatest distress, but no one knew how to stop it. At last, when only one single house remained, the child came home and just said,

"Stop, little pot," and it stopped and gave up cooking, and whosoever wished to return to the town had to eat his way back.

This is a story of a mother who is "too much of a good thing." It hints at how destructive and dangerous that can be. The mother in this story doesn't know how to say stop, and as such the sweet porridge threatens the whole town. It is anger that helps us to find our no, that helps us put our foot down and put an end to that which doesn't serve us or is destructive.

It is perhaps not a coincidence that the destructive action in the story involves a pot that is boiling over. Beth could not allow her own anger into her relationship with her daughter. Where did it go? Perhaps it boiled over in sweetness, filling the room with a sticky ooze that didn't leave room to breathe. Beth was unable to say no to Mindi's inappropriate aggression and therefore her daughter was not getting help in learning to contain these impulses. Some anger on Beth's part would likely have helped Mindi to metabolize her own entirely normal hostility, which likely would have felt relieving to the child.

Angry witchiness can also be in service of protecting our children and vulnerable parts of ourselves. Susan Squire, in an essay entitled "Maternal Bitch," describes how motherhood opened the door to the witch and how this proved, in the end, to be redemptive. "In the house of my first marriage," she begins, when she did not have children, "my inner Bitch was comatose. She was Tinker Bell without Peter, languishing away in a forgotten drawer, losing wattage by the hour—while I congratulated myself for suppressing her so well."[3] We could easily replace "Bitch" here with "shadow." She goes on to explain that her parents had not gotten along. Observing them, she had concluded that "motherhood, whatever else it did, sooner or later made a woman feel put upon."[4] So she decided she would not have children to avoid "activating the Bitch." Although she did manage to avoid children in her first marriage, she and her second husband got pregnant. The Bitch makes her first appearance on the fourth day of the baby's life, as the author and Husband B are struggling with what to do since nursing is not going well. The author begins sobbing hysterically while her husband panics. B offers to go to the store and buy formula.

> "Is that what you call being helpful?" I snarled. "I can't feed her formula!" The Bitch was back to help me fight the good fight. In the most withering tone I could summon, I filled B in on the currently conventional wisdom: Good mothers breast-feed. . . . B waited until I was done. "But isn't some food better than no food?" he said.
>
> Could he be any more annoying? Okay, he was rational, and I was not (that was the annoying part). But guess what? I was no longer hysterical. It occurred to me that annoyance and helplessness are antithetical. . . . Besides, the Bitch wasn't so bad, not at all. She was, to my shock, good company. She was sassy, feisty, not depressed . . . B seemed unfazed by her as he headed out the door.
>
> Fifteen minutes later he returned, clutching a grocery bag and looking smug. . . . "Thanks," I said, "but I—we—don't need it." In B's brief absence, Emily had clamped her mouth on my nipple and was gulping away.[5]

Through motherhood, the author trades in her "nice" false self and reclaims a spirited, resourceful, and ferociously protective shadow side. Her encounter with the witch has allowed her to draw upon deep feminine wisdom so that she can nurse her baby. Her Bitch, like the witches in our story, has an important positive aspect.

WEEPING

Back to our fairy tale. At the demand of the witches, the woman goes to the well with a sieve. Because sieves are used for purifying by sorting, they have come to be associated with self-knowledge, criticism, selection, and choice. The functions of criticism and self-knowledge, however, can become overdeveloped to the point where they become persecutory. Attempting to draw water with a sieve is an image of emotional poverty. This woman, at the moment, has nothing left to give. She is not able to draw upon her well of feeling and relatedness because whatever she tries to scoop up runs right out. When we feel depleted as we mother, attempts to reconnect compassionately with our children can feel like trying to dip a sieve into a well.

The turning point of the tale occurs when the woman sits beside the well and weeps. In fairy tales, when the heroine sits and weeps, unexpected help arrives. Weeping is an acknowledgment of the helplessness of the conscious personality. Such an admission opens you up to guidance from the unconscious. In the story, this help comes from the Spirit of the Well, who instructs the woman how she might be able to make the sieve useful after all. The well can symbolize numinous wisdom from the deep and is often associated with the goddess and the feminine. In Celtic mythology, the well is a place of contact with the other world and frequently contains magic waters.

An intervention from deep, feminine wisdom that arises out of giving ourselves over to our despair can show us how to patch up our wounded ability to share our relatedness. No magic is required, just common, earthy substances that will serve to plug the holes through which our feeling has run. Once we have accomplished this, we can begin the process of banishing the destructive emotion that has overtaken us.

Having been visited by these primal, unmediated feelings, the woman in our story is humbled by the confrontation with the shadow and therefore is able to hear the guidance of the deep, feminine wisdom of the well. We must pass through the shadow before we can come to the creative, renewing depths of the unconscious. In this sense, the confrontation with the witches must precede hearing the Spirit of the Well.

I had my own experience of crying at the well an hour or so after my explosive incident. I took my daughter to the playground and pushed her on the swing. I felt deflated, worn out, tender from the bruising I had inflicted on both of us. Most of the other moms I knew were signing up their two-year-olds for full-time preschool, a step that had felt premature to me. But that day, it occurred to me that perhaps I should send her off after all. If I wasn't the parent I had thought I was for the past two years, perhaps I shouldn't be spending so much time with her. Maybe it was time I brought in the experts and let them do it. But a voice within answered back: "Just because you're not perfect doesn't mean a stranger could do it better." It was a voice that offered me self-acceptance and the difficult road of holding the tension of the opposites. I wasn't a perfect mother. I had a shadow side and could no longer stay identified only with the light. But that didn't mean that the right path was to surrender my claim to invest myself in this endeavor as fully as I could.

The voice that answered me back on the playground told me how to patch up the holes in the sieve. A patched sieve isn't perfect, but maybe it is good enough, and so was I. And it is ultimately a much more courageous and loving act to carry water home in a patched sieve than to have always had a perfect vessel. Growing children don't always do what you want. They disappoint, irritate, and harass. To go on loving them in the face of sometimes hating them—and therefore sometimes hating yourself—is indeed an accomplishment.

Elissa Schappell's angry incident followed a similar pattern. At first, she feels disconnected from her children as a result of her rage. The overwhelming sense of entitlement to her anger, no matter what the cost, gives way to the feeling that she isn't fit to be her children's parent. "I want to cry. . . . It doesn't seem fair that anyone so small should have a mother like me." Eventually, what prevails are her strong feelings of love for her kids despite her anger. She can reassert her claim to her love for her children and identify an urge to repair what was broken.

> Upstairs, I pour myself a glass of red wine and sit on the sofa, still shaking. *But still, I lost it. It wasn't what I did, or didn't do, it was what I could have done. And the truth is, it felt so good to scream, so very good. Even now, after all the books, all the therapy.*
>
> After a few minutes, I get up and go downstairs to check on them. They are both asleep, fingers of moonlight touching their faces. They are perfect.

And suddenly I have this urge to get into bed with them.
I want to curl up around them; I want their arms slung
across my face. . . . I want to whisper in their ears, *Mommy
loves you. Mommy will never hurt you.*[6]

Rage has turned to grief and remorse and has been temporarily banished, but the author is uneasily aware that it can return. Unlike the woman in our fairy tale, she has not been given the magical knowledge she would need to keep the witches out for good, and neither had I on that day at the playground. Can we do anything to banish these destructive feelings permanently? Should we?

SERVING THE WITCH

To answer this question, let's look at another fairy tale that deals with an encounter with the dark, shadowy feminine. In the Russian fairy tale "Vasilisa the Beautiful," Vasilisa's mother has died and left her a magic doll that is able to comfort and help the girl. Her stepmother and stepsisters are cruel, and one night they plot her destruction by sending her out to Baba Yaga's to get some light. Baba Yaga is a dark nature goddess who rules over day and night. Like Kali, she is a fearsome devourer, and the fence around her hut is made of human skulls and bones. Vasilisa travels to her and manages to match wits with her. She serves the witch, and in the end, Baba Yaga bestows on her a gift—a skull with lighted eyes.

Vasilisa goes to the witch at the request of her stepmother but of her own will. Moreover, she carries with her the magic doll, which proves to be protective. Her visit to Baba Yaga is an image of an ego relating at least somewhat consciously with this dark force. At no time does Vasilisa lose her wits or become bespelled by Baba Yaga, though at times she despairs.

The visit to Baba Yaga is fraught with danger and fear but holds the potential of renewal. Baba Yaga is to be feared but also respected, and in other tales in which she appears, she is even sought out by heroes for her wisdom and protective magic. However, despite her positive qualities, you wouldn't necessarily want her moving in with you. In "The

Horned Women," the witches take over the woman's home against her will. This energy comes into the house uninvited and out of control, just as it did for me and Schappell. It is not a conscious descent but a momentary possession by archetypal energies where the conscious personality is spellbound, unable to wrest back control. The witches in "The Horned Women" also carry the same potential for renewal that the shadow always carries and yet they are not in their proper place. From a moral standpoint, the Spirit of the Well is correct that they need to be banished back to their abode in the unconscious.

INTEGRATING RAGE

At the same time, while they ought to return to their original abode, the tale shows us that some part of their energy is integrated and that this is healing. The woman feeds the blood cake to her family. They must ingest or take in some of the food the witches prepared, and this brings them back to life. It is as if the fairy tale is saying that a bit of the food of the dark goddess is healing. If we can integrate some of this shadowy energy, it will renew us. If our unbridled archetypal emotion sucks the very lifeblood from our children and family, then the way to repair is to take this blood and work with it so that it is transformed into something nourishing.

Working with our grief and remorse after such a slip into archetypal fury and transmuting it into an opportunity for repair is like using the blood cake to heal our children. Current parenting research stresses that secure attachment is determined not so much by optimal attunement and responsiveness as by repair.[7]

When we repair, we have the experience of finding ourselves again after we thought we were lost. We are not only repairing the relationship with and for the child but also knitting back together our frayed sense of ourselves, after the devastating experience of our dividedness.

The other injunctions of the Spirit of the Well give us further information about how we are to relate to these shadowy, primitive emotions. To keep this energy in its proper place, we need to accept and value our child's shadow. In the story, the woman must take the water used to wash the children's feet and empty it onto the threshold.

This water, which contains the filth from the feet and would ordinarily be cast off as worthless, is revealed to have magic, protective powers. If we can see what is worthwhile in our children when they are at their very worst, the story tells us, this can help keep the dark goddess in her proper realm.

The woman is also told to leave the cloth that the witches had woven half in and half out of the chest. This web of life that the witches have created is to be caught in between two states, neither in nor out. This curious image suggests holding the tension of the opposites. It guards against being too literal or fixed in one's understanding. The woman must integrate the creation wrought by the witches, but not in a way that contains it entirely. Psychologically, this might mean that we have to own our capacity for rage while avoiding becoming too comfortable with this potential.

Finally, the woman is instructed to secure the door with a great beam. The beam is not an enchantment to keep out the witches but a physical impediment to their reentry. Here, the tale is telling us that it is appropriate to have a strong ego defense against shadow contents. While we ought to integrate and claim some of that fiery energy, we ought to guard against letting it sweep into our psychic homes without restraint. If serving the blood cake and keeping the cloth symbolize being conscious of and working with one's shadow, then barring the door with a beam symbolizes developing one's ego strength. Learning to breathe deeply, practicing self-compassion, or journaling about our feelings are all techniques that may serve as our beam to bar the door against our rage at our children.

In stories of descent to the dark feminine, the heroines all return with a treasure. Vasilisa returns with the fiery skull that has the wisdom of the old witch to burn the stepmother and stepsisters. She carries home with her consciousness (light) and aggression she lacked before her visit to the dark goddess. In our story, the treasure is the witch's mantle, which symbolizes protection, mystery, and power. To wear a witch's mantle would be to assume some of her power and authority—in other words, to be in a creative relationship with this archetypal energy without being consumed or possessed by it.

When we integrate the shadow, something is lost, but something else is always gained. C. G. Jung wrote that the goal of individuation is wholeness, not perfection. Recognizing our shadow causes us to lose the belief that we are basically nice people, as Fay Weldon points out, but brings in its place the opportunity for us to accept ourselves more fully and completely in all of our imperfect wholeness.

Giving up the ideal of the all-perfect, all-loving mother is frequently very difficult for mothers in our culture because the feminine shadow has been so deeply repressed. The idealization of the "bright" side of motherhood has a long and illustrious history, going back, of course, at least as far as the cult of the Blessed Virgin. It is alive and well today in popular culture, where every new generation of mothers is exposed to dogmatic parenting books. We idealize the notion of blissful unity and don't want to admit that conflict and friction are also part of a relationship. Our culture overvalues an idealized, unrealistic set of expectations about ourselves and our experience of motherhood while the shadow side—which is dark, unruly, even frightening, but also filled with authenticity and vitality—cannot be related to consciously.

A mother interviewed by psychiatrist Rozsika Parker expresses her experience with this.

> I had no idea how much anger and hatred there was inside me. I had always been a nice little person, afraid and rather submissive. I had been in therapy but it didn't give me access to all the feelings of rage and anger at being left out, disliked and resented that surfaced after Diane was born. I've had to work that through myself. Motherhood has made me come to terms with it. I feel now that I can separate from the children a bit more and begin to lead something of my own life, because I have looked the enemy in the face and seen it was me. All the aggression that I hated in my mother and hated in Diane, I can now locate in myself—and I have somehow united with it.[8]

Wholeness requires that we consciously relate to shadow. We cannot split off the objectionable parts of ourselves without sacrificing growth and consciousness. Increased self-knowledge is perhaps the greatest boon you receive after an encounter with your shadow. This, in turn, brings with it greater authenticity and substance. "How can I be substantial if I fail to cast a shadow?" asks Jung. "I must have a dark side also if I am to be whole."[9]

Questions for Reflection for Embodying Darkness

1. Has there ever been a time when you have genuinely lost it with your kids? What happened, and how did you feel afterward? Have you ever told anyone about it?

2. Once the witches have entered, the woman is unable to speak or move because she is under the witches' spell. When we are overcome with strong emotions, it can feel as though we are under a spell as we watch ourselves doing things we wouldn't ordinarily do and experience ourselves as unable to stop ourselves. Has this happened to you recently? What did you do? How did you feel afterward?

3. The mother in the story receives help from the Spirit of the Well. When you are exhausted, spent, or irritable, what inner resources do you call on to help you reestablish equilibrium?

4. The motif of trying to scoop up water with a sieve frequently occurs in fairy tales. It is an evocative image of emotional depletion, perhaps. When have you felt as though you were trying to draw up water with a sieve when interacting with your children? How does this feel?

5. The mother is able to bring her children back to life by feeding them the cake the witches made. If you lose your temper with your children, what do you usually do to repair the rupture?

6. The mistress is told to bar the door with a great beam to keep the witches out. Most parents can relate to becoming enraged with their children, and most try their hardest to avoid doing so. What techniques have you tried to avoid losing your temper with your kids? Have any of them worked? In your opinion, why have or haven't they worked?

7. When you have gotten angry with your children, how do you go about repairing the relationship?

PART III

SURFACING

CHAPTER 7

Claiming Transcendence

Without knowing it man is
always concerned with god.

C. G. JUNG
IN C. G. JUNG SPEAKING

aving survived her journey to the strange world at the bottom of the well and successfully completed myriad trials, the heroine in "The Two Caskets" returns home with rich gifts. Because she was wise and hardworking and listened to the various denizens of this strange land, the cats helped her by instructing her to choose the plain black casket. When she opened the little box inside her henhouse home, gold and jewels spilled out, filling up the room. When we remain open to our inner life as we navigate the trials of mothering, we will also gain great riches—priceless wisdom and an abiding experience of wholeness that gives us a firm foundation in the world. Such wisdom is no small thing. It will alter the very nature of our relationship with life—and ourselves.

Developing a mature spirituality is an important part of growing into psychological wholeness. It will require us to discern which of those values that have been bequeathed to us by our families or our culture we wish to embrace and which we choose to jettison. Developing a mature spirituality does not necessarily imply participating in formal religion. It does mean having the courage to examine our values and beliefs and to come to an understanding of our significance and place in the universe. Motherhood offers us an excellent opportunity to make sense of our place in the cosmos, as well as a way to reexamine those values according to which we have been living.

REORIENTATION OF VALUES

Whereas before children, we may have been very invested in making money or seeking career success, we sometimes find that being a mother shifts our center of gravity, altering us irrevocably in an altogether different direction. For some women, such a reorientation of values may come easily and, indeed, might be welcome. For others, it can be experienced as a painful relinquishing of what we had held most dear. If we are oriented to the world of work and achievement and used to receiving praise and recognition for our accomplishments in this arena, the very different demands made on us by motherhood can feel like a diminishment or even a defeat.

My client Cynthia had been a successful businesswoman before having children. By the time she was in her late twenties, she had already started her climb up the corporate ladder. With degrees from impressive universities and various awards and recognitions, Cynthia had been a high-flying achiever before she became a mother. When her first child sustained a minor injury while in the care of a nanny when Cynthia was traveling on business, she was forced to rethink her priorities. She quit her job and restructured her life so that she could be a stay-at-home mom.

She recalls that she found the loss of professional status disorienting and devastating. "I didn't know who I was anymore," she told me. "I was shocked at how quickly I became irrelevant to my former employees and colleagues." Used to excelling at whatever she set her mind to, Cynthia assumed that taking care of her baby would be a no-brainer. She was stunned by how difficult she found it. "At work, I could close a million-dollar sale, but at home, I could barely get through breakfast. It would be 7:30 in the morning, and it would already feel like it had been a long day," she said.

Cynthia's experience brought to mind an Algonquin legend that speaks to how parenting can feel like a defeat.

GLOOSCAP AND THE BABY

Glooscap was a mighty warrior and possessor of magical powers. He had saved the world from an evil frog monster and defeated demons, giants, and witches. He had subdued all of his enemies and felt himself to be great indeed!

One day, he boasted to an old woman that he was invincible. "I am so great and powerful," he said, "that there is no one who can defeat me."

The old woman laughed and warned Glooscap not to be too certain. "There is one foe you've never faced," she told him.

Glooscap demanded to see this mighty being, so the old woman went into the next room and brought back a little baby. She set him on the floor, where he sat cooing and sucking his thumb. Glooscap smiled at such a silly prank. Why, this great foe was only a small child!

"Baby, come to me now!" he commanded. But the baby just sat cooing and drooling. Glooscap tried to charm the baby by imitating a beautiful bird song. The baby smiled, but he didn't move.

Glooscap was not accustomed to being treated in such a manner. He became angry and roared his command that the baby come to him. This made the baby cry. He cried and cried. Glooscap recited all of the most powerful incantations he knew. He said the spells for raising the dead, but the baby only cried louder. Glooscap recited an incantation to banish demons, but the baby's wails rose to a deafening pitch.

At last, Glooscap, the great and powerful warrior, had to admit defeat. He strode away, vanquished. The baby went back to cooing.

The mighty Glooscap is no match for a baby! Conquering foes in the outer world requires directedness, aggression, and boldness. Being with children requires something altogether different. As a result, women such as Cynthia, who have lived heroically before having children, may find motherhood especially difficult. Babies, young children, and teenagers challenge our sense of control. The skills valued in professional life don't necessarily prepare us for the flexibility, emotional regulation, and careful attunement to another person required for successful parenting of kids and teens. If we have defeated the giants and witches of the academic or professional world, we may be very used to feeling capable in the face of challenge. For some women who fit this description, having children can indeed mean finally meeting their match.

DEFEAT

With its many defeats, motherhood can be an experience that initiates us into an encounter with limitation, putting us in contact with that which is larger than we are. When we are defeated, an aspect of us dies. Motherhood will require our former self to be sacrificed so that we can be reborn into a larger version of ourselves. Such a death is always painful, and most of us resist. We may feel comfortable with our lives, achievements, and interests. We have created our little kingdom and do not wish to have it overthrown.

Before having children, you may have felt that you could control many aspects of your daily life. Even if you had a stressful job or other hardships, you likely felt that you had at least some ability to decide what to pay attention to or how to spend your time. When children enter the picture, there is so much we can't control. Whether your child is a dawdling toddler or a recalcitrant teenager, you find yourself in some sense responsible for another being over whom you do not have total control or authority. This offers many opportunities to feel defeated.

Finding ourselves "defeated" by motherhood in this manner can be shattering. When we want to do our very best at everything we try, how awful to discover that the most important job we have is the one we can't do to our satisfaction! For some women, the realization that parenting is a struggle is so difficult that it can cause them to disconnect from their children and turn away from their role as a mother. However, if we can bear this defeat, it can enlarge and enliven us. It can be an experience that helps us to grow beyond the limits of our conscious personality. It can penetrate our defenses, upend our carefully guarded sense of ourselves, rend asunder what we thought we knew about our lives—and in these ways, open us up to wider perspectives and greatly increased self-knowledge. In the words of poet

Rainer Maria Rilke, we grow "by being defeated, decisively, by constantly greater beings."[1] Facing defeat, therefore, can usher us into an encounter with our depths. Defeat is rarely pleasant, but such experiences help us grow roots into an embodied sense of meaning and purpose. Defeat is how we encounter soul.

Such a defeat is, in its essence, a religious experience in that it instructs us in humility and teaches us that we must submit to a greater will. In a letter written toward the end of his life, C. G. Jung wrote that "God is the name by which I designate all things which cross my willful path violently and recklessly, all things which upset my subjective views, plans, and intentions, and change the course of my life for better or worse."[2] When our ego desires are thwarted at every turn, this is, in effect, an encounter with the divine.

Since the way to wholeness is often at odds with the narrow path preferred by our conscious personality, we may need to experience a defeat to be opened up to the larger possibilities in store for us. Jung famously wrote that "the experience of the Self is always a defeat for the ego,"[3] by which he meant that an encounter with the inner guiding self will always be humbling to our conscious personality. The kind of ego defeat often experienced while mothering can make us receptive to inner guidance and wisdom.

This was certainly the case with Cynthia. In our work together, she explored what it was like for her to have her expectations for herself and her life so suddenly upended. Throughout early adulthood, she had only ever imagined for herself a life of professional accomplishment, and it was for this that she had prepared herself. At first, the loss of status and structure plunged her into a dark time in which she struggled to find value in the daily, mind-numbing duties of parenthood. As she adjusted, however, she began to find mothering deeply meaningful. She now recalls those years at home with her children as some of the most important—and fulfilling—times of her life.

When her children were both in school, Cynthia felt it right to go back to work, but this time, she knew she would need a job that engaged her creativity, curiosity, and need for meaning. "Those years at home reshaped my expectations for myself," Cynthia said. "I couldn't see going back to a corporate environment where it would be just about profit." Cynthia used her considerable skills to start a nonprofit that helps women find their way back into the workforce after taking time out to parent. It is work that she finds deeply engaging—and it also allows her flexibility so that she can attend her daughters' sports games. "I'm not the person I was before I had children," she told me in our first session. "The things I care about are different." For Cynthia, submitting to the defeats of motherhood brought a reorientation of values and a deep sense of meaning and purpose.

RELATIONSHIP TO THE INFINITE

A reconsideration of our values might be one of the gifts of motherhood that contribute to the development of mature spirituality. But there is an even more fundamental way that motherhood can connect us with our spiritual center. Regardless of religious orientation or adherence to particular belief systems, our sense of our place in the universe is dependent in part on our having a felt relationship with something larger than ourselves. "The decisive question for man is: Is he related to something infinite or not?" Jung wrote in his autobiography. "That is the telling question of his life."[4] Our role in the creation and nurture of a new being places us squarely in the flow of life's inexhaustible continuance and puts us in proximity to this miracle. Parenthood, which connects us to the past through the ancestors and to the future through our children, can be an important part of this relationship with something infinite. This experience can open us up to a sense of connectedness with and responsibility for our community, our world, and our planet. In this way, motherhood may help solidify the feeling of being part of a larger, universal plan.

The Annunciation—the moment when archangel Gabriel tells Mary she will conceive and give birth to Jesus—has been a favorite subject of artists through the centuries, and I always love these paintings. Mary often looks awe-stricken, frightened, humbled—and sometimes even wary or disgusted! It is an image of a shattering encounter with the divine, one that recognizes the power of motherhood to set our life on a different course—one informed by contact with transpersonal energy. Our personal, modern-day annunciation of pregnancy usually involves peeing on a stick, but the life-altering feelings that accompany a positive test result often serve to remind us of our connection with something larger.

For some women, giving birth is an indescribably numinous event that can also give us a sense of being connected to something infinite. It often fills us with the joy, terror, and awe that are the hallmarks of a deeply spiritual experience. Religions the world over have given expression to the momentous mystery of the birth experience. Some of the most beautiful stories from mythology and religion concern the miraculous birth of the divine child, whether that is Buddha, Jesus, or Krishna. Describing her daughter's birth, Rachel Cusk eloquently notes the change in the fabric of time that she experienced. "Some transfer of significance has occurred: I feel it, feel the air move, feel time begin to pour down a new tributary," she explains. "The world itself adjusts."[5]

Much of the impetus behind the modern natural childbirth movement derives from a deep-seated desire to restore sacredness to the experience. For many women, unmedicated labor and birth are opportunities to experience themselves via the archetype of the creatrix and to make contact with this powerful aspect of the feminine. Many women may not want to pursue natural childbirth, or cannot for medical reasons. Even a highly medicalized procedure such as a Cesarean section can be experienced as numinous and sacred, however.

I recall my own daughter's birth by Cesarean. I lay pinned on the table, aware of the coldness and brightness of the room and the strange sensation of tugging at my abdomen below the blue drape. It was odd, frightening, and antiseptic, and the hushed voices of the doctors and electronic noises of equipment were dampened and distorted as if they originated a long way off. The tugging ceased, and the room grew expectantly quiet. And then she cried. It was such an indescribably sweet little cry. Until that moment, she had seemed hypothetical. Now, here she was, real and squirming and miraculously alive—a new being.

Newborns retain this glow of the miraculous. When my daughter was a few days old, I began to notice her smell. No one had warned me about how newborn baby girls smell. It was something like a freshly mown meadow in springtime, but even more glorious. It was as if, having just come through the veil from the "other side," she still shimmered with some of the numinosity of the infinite. William Wordsworth expressed this beautifully in his famous lines:

> Not in entire forgetfulness,
> And not in utter nakedness,
> But trailing clouds of glory do we come
> From God, who is our home.[6]

If we give birth, that experience may be filled with ecstasy, pride, joy, or other positive experiences. If we have expectations for a birth experience that are not met, or if there is an emergency and our life or the life of the baby is in danger, we may feel terror, grief, anger, and regret. In either case, childbirth and the ensuing weeks of new motherhood are likely to put us in contact with the thin edge between our everyday world and the infinite. After such an experience, it can be difficult to remain unaware of how we are connected to something larger—whether that larger thing is the miracle of new life or the terror of the void. In either case, a birth experience can serve to relativize our ordinary, everyday life by making explicit the vastness of the context in which we are embedded. Becoming awake to the infinite in which we all exist—though we often don't notice it—can be an important part of developing a mature spirituality.

New motherhood is not the only time that you will feel challenged to understand your place in the cosmos. As our children grow older and get ready to leave home, we are likely to feel acutely the cold chill of mortality seeping back to us from the future. When your children become adults and then parents themselves, you experience the inexorable turning of the great wheel. You recall the tiny newborn you bathed in a tub placed in the kitchen sink as you watch her now, fully grown, going out into the world to meet her own fate, and you know yourself to be part of life's great round. Everyone, of course, will be faced with mortality whether or not they are parents. But motherhood in particular connects us with the cycle of death and birth in a compelling and intimate fashion.

MEANING AND PURPOSE

For my client Laura, motherhood connected her with "something infinite." It imbued her life with meaning and redeemed her suffering. Laura had experienced significant physical, sexual, and emotional abuse as a child. When I first met her, she sat with me for the full hour without ever once making eye contact. Her arms and legs were covered with horizontal scars as a result of cutting. She told me that she had come to therapy because she had been thinking carefully about things and had decided that her life was one of suffering without any redeeming meaning. She had determined that suicide would be a rational choice. When she told this to her boyfriend, he had begged her to seek therapy before carrying out any plans, and she agreed. She admitted that, though she couldn't find any reason not to commit suicide, there was a significant part of her that didn't want to die.

In the next months, I worked painstakingly to gain her trust. Over time, she shared the story of her childhood with me. She continued to avoid eye contact with me except for the briefest moments. One evening, she stepped into my office, sat down, and looked at me. I immediately felt that something had shifted. "I'm pregnant," she said. Laura announced right away that this took suicide off the table for moral reasons—for the time being. She felt that killing herself now that she was pregnant would, in effect, be killing the baby that was growing inside her. In her opinion, this was not something that she had the right to do.

To myself, I worried that the pregnancy would be difficult for Laura, given her earlier traumas, and this was, indeed, a difficult time. But Laura also felt a strong sense of duty to her growing child that tied her to life in a healthy way. She became meticulous about what she ate, for example, to ensure that the baby got proper nutrition. She was able to care for her growing baby in a way she had never been able to care for herself alone.

Though she had immediately assumed that she would give the child up for adoption, Laura admitted to me one evening that she was beginning to wonder about keeping it. This was a significant confession. Even after learning she was pregnant, Laura had not surrendered the possibility of suicide. The pregnancy merely took it off the table temporarily. However, deciding to keep the child would, I knew, mean committing herself to life. It was as if the baby growing inside her was an expression of life's eternal will toward its own furtherance. As the pregnancy took hold, so did her determination toward life. As the growing baby took over more of her body and demanded more from her, Laura's commitment to meet its needs grew in kind.

In the end, Laura and her boyfriend kept the baby. Though she had been very afraid she would not be a good mother because of her childhood history of abuse, Laura found that she took to mothering quite naturally. She adored her son and took pleasure in caring for him. Of course, there were dark times when she felt overwhelmed. The thoughts of suicide and self-harm did not go away magically. Because she had no model for appropriate parenting, she felt she needed to read a library of parenting books. And yet she could also appreciate that she often knew the right thing to do even without consulting her books.

To recognize that these ancient nurturing instincts flowed through her unimpeded despite her never having received such care herself seemed nothing short of miraculous to Laura. This new experience of herself shifted the center of gravity in her personality. It gave her confidence in herself, but it did something even more profound. It connected her with the world. She had always experienced herself as standing outside the pale of normal human existence—an experience not uncommon for survivors of profound trauma. Now she found herself connected to her child and to other mothers—those around her and those who had come before her.

Becoming a mother connected her with the world in other ways as well. When her son was a toddler, he was diagnosed with a rare medical condition. She became a fierce advocate on his behalf. She was able to locate and mobilize essential resources. This young woman who hadn't been able to make eye contact now grew skilled at wrangling physicians and insurance company representatives. She found online support groups for other families suffering from the condition and became an important part of these communities. Eventually advocacy became her life's work. Even after her son no longer needed treatment or support, Laura continued to work to bring attention to the condition and to raise money for research and treatment on behalf of other families.

For Laura, the experience of motherhood connected her with "something infinite." It gave her a sense of meaning and purpose beyond herself. Though being a mother is certainly not the only way one can become connected with something larger, caring for children is, in essence, a way of tending to the future—even a future we will not see. For many of us, it will be a significant way that we contribute to the ongoing project of humanity, allowing life to move forward through us and beyond us. In this way, we become a part of something incomprehensibly vast.

THE MINNOWS AND THE WHALE

There is a Polynesian expression that eloquently captures the dual nature of being: standing on a whale, fishing for minnows. Most of the time, we spend our lives focused on the little, quotidian problems that fill our days—the minnows. Only rarely do we catch a glimpse of the vast, awe-filled, transcendent reality that undergirds our existence—the whale. Jung noted that we are always living in two worlds: the everyday world of our senses and an eternal world.

Motherhood may be unique in its ability to allow us to oscillate between these two levels of awareness—the ordinary and the infinite, the minnows and the whale. The mundane, tedious nature of many of the daily tasks of mothering plant us firmly in the ordinary physical level of awareness much of the time. However, these stretches of tedium may be punctuated by frequent jolts of awareness of something from quite a different level. We have a dizzying glimpse of how quickly time is passing. We experience extremes of emotion, such as rage or joy, that knock us out of our everyday awareness. We are stunned by the radical otherness of our child. A beautiful story from Hindu mythology captures this characteristic oscillation between these two states, showing how ancient and universal this experience is.

LORD KRISHNA EATS MUD

When the great god Krishna was a toddler, he lived with his foster mother, Yashoda, and his older brother Balarama. One day, Balarama complained to his mother that Krishna was eating mud. Fearful for his safety, Yashoda took Krishna's hand and scolded him sternly.

"Why have you been eating mud?" she asked him. Krishna looked up at her, his eyes seeming wide with fear. When he denied eating any mud, Yashoda demanded that he open his mouth so that she could see.

The boy opened his mouth wide, and his mother looked inside. There she saw the sun, the moon, and the stars. She saw the entirety of the earth with its mountains, lakes, and oceans. She saw all of creation, the universe, fire, and air, the swirling constellations. She saw the very fabric of time stretching out in all directions.

After a moment, Krishna cast the divine power of illusion over his mother in the form of maternal affection. Her memory was immediately erased. She took little Krishna on her lap, as her heart brimmed with intense love.

This ancient story captures the dual nature of being with young children. One moment, we are firmly in this world of adult consciousness, taking care of chores and chasing after a child who has just put a LEGO in his mouth. The next moment, we have been transported into immediate contact with the divine and infinite because of something our child has said or done. Like Glooscap, Yashoda fancies herself as the one in charge of her young son. And just as with Glooscap, her sense of certainty and control is punctured by an encounter with her child.

I first read this story when my son was an unruly toddler like Krishna. He was always putting things in his mouth, and I was often demanding that he open up so that I could check that he wasn't in danger of choking. "What's in your mouth?" I would demand of him frequently when I suspected him. On any day, I might ask him this several times. ("Teeth!" he would sometimes answer.) Then something would happen that would suddenly knock me out of my everyday orientation. I would have a vertiginous sense of how quickly he was growing up. In an instant, I was aware of the sweet fragility of life and how swiftly it passes. My heart would ache from the poignancy of it—an awareness of the whale—and then that moment would be over and I would be back to wiping up spilled macaroni and cheese off the kitchen floor. I would be back to the minnows.

Author and mom Polly Berrien Berends had a dream that spoke to these two aspects of reality and the embodied ordinariness that is an inescapable part of a mother's spiritual journey:

> *Once I had a dream in which I was to receive a diploma as*
> *a spiritual teacher or guide of some sort. There were two of us*
> *being presented with such a certificate at the time. The other was*
> *a man—Swamibabagururishiroshirabbisoandso. He wore long*
> *colorful robes and had a fist full of degrees and papers. To receive*
> *his diploma he only had to step forward and present himself*
> *with his long titles, flowing robes, and abundant credentials.*
> *But before me there stood and enormous mountain of laundry.*
> *To receive my diploma I would first have to climb over this huge*
> *heap of laundry.[7]*

The dream expresses a vital bit of wisdom. Spiritual awareness by itself can lead to inflation and an unhealthy disconnection with everyday reality. Transcendent awareness must be grounded in the imperfect, ordinary existence if it is to be more than a beautiful defense against our very human vulnerability. Alternating between these two perspectives—the everyday and the infinite—we become accustomed to seeing ourselves both as an ordinary person who has three loads of laundry to do, and as a link in the vast chain of being. Our actions can take on a dual significance as we live life on the familiar plane of everyday reality—minnows—while also becoming aware of the transcendent under our very feet—whale.

INTEGRATION

Motherhood, then, can invite us to ground our spiritual awareness in everyday, embodied reality, asking us to give expression to both aspects of ourselves. Such integration can result in a deeply felt sense of meaning and purpose, as we experience our daily lives connected in a profound way to the resonant hum of the cosmos.

Motherhood ushered in such a sense of integration for Catholic activist and journalist Dorothy Day. Born in 1897, Day was a founder of the Catholic Worker movement and worked tirelessly for social justice for the poor until her death in 1980. She is currently under consideration for possible canonization by the Catholic Church.

As a young woman, however, her religious life was far ahead of her. In her late teens, she left college and moved to lower Manhattan, where she wrote for several Socialist publications, got arrested and jailed for picketing for women's suffrage, and consorted with Eugene O'Neill and several prominent communists. She lived a bohemian life, having affairs with various men. When she became pregnant at age twenty-four, she had an abortion and believed herself to be sterile as a result. She was briefly married, but the relationship ended unhappily. By her late twenties she had a new lover and found herself longing to have a child.

Despite her fears that she was infertile, Day did become pregnant. Throughout her pregnancy, Day found herself increasingly drawn to the church. She began to pray daily. The conviction grew in her to become baptized in the Catholic Church and to have her child baptized, but she knew this would mean the end of her relationship with her common-law husband and the baby's father.

It was becoming a mother that opened Day up to ecstatic experience, finally cracking her open to the awareness of the infinite. "No human creature could receive or contain so vast a flood of love and joy as I often felt after the birth of my child. With this came the need to worship, to adore,"[8] wrote Day in her autobiography. The birth of her child became for Day the deciding factor that led her, at last, to become baptized as a Catholic. Becoming a mother sharpened and focused Day's religious convictions as well as her political and social activism.

CHRONOS AND KAIROS

Time is the chief medium through which we experience an oscillation between the dual aspects of existence when we parent. The expression "the minutes drag, but the years fly" sums up this sentiment. When we are parenting young children, we may feel time *both* flying and dragging in an alternating fashion several times in a single day. When my two were toddlers, I recall thinking in terms of half-hour chunks of time, as in, *How can I get through the next half hour?* And yet I was frequently overcome with emotion when I realized how quickly time was passing.

Babies and young children grow so quickly that we are suddenly aware in a painful and visceral way of the passage of time. It is as if we can suddenly feel the spinning of the earth on its axis. Before I had children, time was like a river I swam in but could barely sense its movement. There were those moments of realizing that some past event had occurred longer ago than seemed possible, and this brought the startling realization that time was indeed passing. But most of the time, the river was so deep and broad that I barely noticed its gentle flow.

Once I had children, my relationship with time changed. For great chunks of every day, I wondered how I would survive until bedtime. I hungered for sleep and time to myself. Just as fiercely, I wanted those days to last. Their childhoods seemed like a swiftly flowing river that rushed away from me toward the future too quickly.

The Greeks personified time as the great Titan Chronos. In Greco-Roman mosaics, he is portrayed as unceasingly turning the wheel of the zodiac. Chronos quietly stalks us as we parent, whispering to us of time's passing as we pack away the holiday decorations and give away the outgrown clothes. But the Greeks had another image of time—that of Kairos, the god of the fleeting moment. Motherhood is full of such moments of kairos as well—when we enter a timeless state with our child as we share a walk in the woods on a sun-dappled autumn afternoon, or when we give ourselves over to the pleasure of watching our sleeping newborn as we hold her in our lap. If Chronos is the god of the ordinary, everyday awareness and the minnows, Kairos speaks to our ability to make contact with the infinite and the whale.

In her book *Maternal Desire*, psychologist Daphne de Marneffe writes beautifully of one such Kairos moment.

> On a still morning when everyone else went down to
> the park, I sat alone with the baby, listening to his newborn
> breaths as he slept on my lap and later his snuffling, hungry
> sucks. I could hear the cooing of the mourning doves
> perched on the telephone wire above the street, and the
> crows' caws farther down the hill. Out the window were
> drooping sunlit spider webs the children would later inspect
> and destroy, and butterflies, whose darting bright lives were
> measured in days. I could not have been more full; life could
> not have been more sweet. And at the same time, there was
> also that ache, at "the rustling of the grains of sand as they
> slid lightly away," and at my baby's sleeping breath; that ache
> of beauty and longing and time and the unbearable fragility
> and surpassing preciousness of each moment.[9]

De Marneffe uses the term *nostalgia for the present* to describe that in-the-moment awareness of the quiet slipping of the grains of sand. While this ache is often more intense when our children are babies and toddlers because they are growing and changing so quickly, it never leaves us all together. Sentinel times in our children's lives remind us of the inexorable flow of time and recall us to kairos.

Kristin van Ogtrop is an essayist, magazine editor, and mother. In her essay "Attila the Honey I'm Home," she catalogs how her work, though demanding and stressful, is easier for her than being at home with her two small boys. Much of her difficulty has to do with time—van Ogtrop spends most of her life in chronos and feels comfortable there. She resists dropping into kairos, although she poignantly acknowledges an awareness of the slipping grains of sand.

> This, I fear, is how it will be: I will love my children, but
> my love for them will be imperfect, damaged by my rigid

personality and the demands of my work. I will never be able to share the surprise they feel when they find a cicada in the grass, because stopping to marvel at the cicada means I will miss my morning train. . . . The years will pass, Owen and Hugo will grow, and I will continue to dream about the time when I can walk in the front door and feel relaxed.

I will long for a time when I will never yell at my kids just because I am late. . . .

Because before I know it, my boys will be grown. The house will be spotless, and so will I: nice, calm, both at work and at home. Four little feet jumping on the bed will be a distant memory. And things like cicadas will have lost their magic, and my children will be gone for good.[10]

To be a mother, then, is to live with a burning awareness of the passage of time. Some women find themselves overcome with a desire for another baby in part as a way to put off the inevitable reckoning with chronos. If there is a new baby on the horizon, there's more life ahead. Another child can allow us to suspend ourselves for a few brief years in the extended youth that pregnancy and nursing brings. On the other hand, to declare ourselves done is to round life's corner and see ahead the long home stretch, conceding to life's inexorable onward rush toward aging and eventual death. Eventually, of course, there is always a last baby, whether it is the first or the fifth. With a heave of primal sorrow, we turn to see that part of our lives receding swiftly into the past. The mourning cannot be deferred any longer. Whether we let ourselves feel it as the infant toys go out to the curb, or whether we steel ourselves against it until the day they leave for college, grief is present from the very beginning and never really leaves us.

Time is that to which we must inevitably submit, though most of us spend much of our lives attempting to avoid awareness of this fact. Parenting, with its frequent wrenching reminders of our children's fleeting youth, makes the inexorability of time's passage much harder to ignore.

A yet more momentous passage awaits us—that day our children leave home. "Eventually, the cosmologists assure us, our sun and all suns will consume their fuel, violently explode and then become cold and dark. Matter itself will evaporate into the void and the universe will become desolate for the rest of time." So begins Michael Gerson's 2013 essay about his son leaving for college published in the *Washington Post*.

He continues:

> This was the general drift of my thoughts as my wife
> and I dropped off my eldest son as a freshman at college. I
> put on my best face. But it is the worst thing that time has
> done to me so far. That moment at the dorm is implied
> at the kindergarten door, at the gates of summer camp, at
> every ritual of parting and independence. But it comes as
> surprising as a thief, taking what you value most.[11]

"It is the worst thing that time has done to me so far." Chronos inevitably betrays us. No matter what bargain we think we have struck with life, he wins in the end. While having children creates a sense of expansiveness, of new life branching off of the generative trunk of our being, when our children leave home, we are reminded that we must relinquish our hold on the future. It will be here when we are gone.

When our child grows up and moves away, we see her moving on to life's stage, expansive horizons spreading out in every direction. Simultaneously we have an awareness that our vast horizons stretch out behind us. What lies ahead we know to be finite. Our greatest and most meaningful adventure has now drawn to a close, and this is such a momentous, irrevocable, and abrupt end that, as Gerson writes, "planets are thrown off their axes."[12]

Like so much of parenting, our child leaving home is a confrontation with finitude and limitation. We understand that our time with them is limited. Our place in their lives is limited and will be even more so going forward. And we experience viscerally that the time remaining to us is limited. When confronted in this way, with life's inevitable limitation, we may respond by distracting ourselves from this painful knowledge. If we allow it, however, this experience can sharpen our focus on what matters most, propelling us to live according to deeply held values.

Mothering holds our feet to the fire of our mortality. It reveals to us the fast turning of the gears of time. In this way, it can plunge us into daily contact with what Jung called the "central fire"—an immediate sense of our ground of being, the world of the eternal. For this reason, motherhood can be a great spiritual teacher, inviting us into a deeper relationship with that "something infinite."

Questions for Reflection for Claiming Transcendence

1. Glooscap hadn't ever met an enemy he couldn't defeat—until he encountered a baby. For some women, taking care of an infant comes naturally, but others of us feel more like Glooscap. Has work outside the home felt easier for you than mothering? How so? How have you felt defeated in your mothering experience?

2. Nothing that Glooscap does works to make the baby obey him. Parenting requires us to cultivate a different attitude than we might need when addressing career challenges. What attitudes have you found were unhelpful or even counterproductive as you have parented? How did you come to realize that these attitudes weren't serving you?

3. If you had an experience of being overwhelmed in the course of mothering, how did you respond to this? How did it change you? How have your values shifted or changed since you became a parent?

4. Both Glooscap and Yashoda find themselves bested by a young child. In what ways have your children made you aware of limitations you didn't know you had before?

5. Yashoda goes from experiencing a very ordinary parenting moment to a moment of extreme spiritual awareness. Something like this can happen to us frequently, especially when we have small children. Have you had an experience of oscillating between such extremes as you care for your children? If so, how has this experience shifted your perspective?

6. Yashoda is given a glimpse of the infinite through her child. How has your relationship with time changed since having children? How has this changed how you think about your spirituality?

7. How has your experience of spirituality changed since becoming a mom? How has your relationship to time changed?

CHAPTER 8

Claiming Creativity

Only in our creative acts do we step forth into the
light and see ourselves whole and complete.

C. G. JUNG
COLLECTED WORKS, VOL. 8

A ll kinds of rich treasures fall out of the little casket the heroine
brings home from her sojourn at the bottom of the well. Might
one of them be creativity? Motherhood and creativity have a
complicated relationship. Whether we work in a creative field or have
a creative practice that is important to us, the arrival of children in our
lives is likely to dampen our artistic aspirations significantly. When
we have young children, the lack of sleep and the constant physical
demands may make it nearly impossible for us to find time to pursue
a creative activity. As our children get older, managing their schedules
and driving them to activities can take up much of our time. We may
find it especially difficult to make time for a creative pursuit if we
are also working outside the home. Our children, partners, and jobs
will often take priority over other things, leaving our need for self-
expression far down the list—and often unsatisfied.

THE BURDEN OF MOTHERHOOD

Throughout history, women's artistic endeavors were often
actively discouraged. Those women who did pursue creative
paths most often did not have children. Though there are some

notable exceptions—Clara Schumann, the great German pianist of the Romantic era, had eight children—most accomplished women painters, novelists, and musicians were not mothers, leading one to wonder whether creative generativity and parenthood are more or less irreconcilable. Ironically, the Impressionist painter Mary Cassatt, renowned for her tender and astutely observed paintings of mother and child, had decided early in her life that marriage would be incompatible with her ambition to be a painter.

Happily, much has changed for women in the past half century or so, making it easier for us to pursue creative ambitions, although being able to devote oneself to creative pursuits even part time requires a degree of economic stability that not all mothers have. If we as mothers are working to support our families while also tending to children, it may not be possible for us to make room for creative practices. The ability to live the life of a creative is a privilege, indeed. Even for women with such privilege and with societal changes that support women's professional endeavors, however, it continues to be difficult to be a mother and a creative person. For American poet Diane Mehta, the arrival of children temporarily asphyxiated her artistic life.

> Most women writers with children fight their inner
> conflict quietly and slide in a few hours when they can, and
> make time for what's possible. But some, like myself, just
> give it up. . . . For the first three years of my son's life, I did
> virtually everything: I quit my job, nursed, made playdates,
> read to him for a half hour nightly, then coaxed him slowly
> to sleep. Over the course of nearly seven years, I had stopped
> writing, retreated from most friendships, and had become,
> in retrospect, an embittered zombie, walking through life
> and parenthood with an unease that seemed uncomfortably
> counter to the cheer-emoting mothers that wheeled their
> giant double strollers around the baby-making machine that
> is Park Slope.[1]

How many symphonies were never composed because mothering took a woman away from her art? How many paintings never painted, or poems or novels never written? The writer Barbara Kingsolver tells us that the poet Lucille Clifton was once asked why her poems were so short, to which she replied, "I have six children, and a memory that can hold about twenty lines until the end of the day."[2] The collective loss to the world of artistic treasures as a result of motherhood must surely be staggering.

Yet motherhood has a way of introducing us to ourselves. As we come to know ourselves better and become better acquainted with our hard-won resilience, we may find ourselves compelled to give voice to our authenticity in some way. Motherhood savagely reorganizes our priorities. For some women, this may mean claiming space for a creative endeavor at the expense of other less important activities that once took up room in their lives.

After I finished analytic training, it became clear how crucial it was for me to write this book. Ever since I was a child, I have wanted to write. As a young adult considering a career, I set that desire aside as impractical. I also felt that writers were exceptionally talented—something I couldn't imagine claiming for myself. For the next twenty years, I lived my life, developing a career, getting a couple of graduate degrees, marrying, having children, and entering analytic training. My desire to write never left me, and I have drafts of more than one unfinished novel tucked away in a closet. But I never allowed myself to commit to writing seriously.

The desire to write burned like hot embers carefully banked at the back of my life for decades. Alongside this desire was the fear of inadequacy that kept me from really claiming my wish to be a writer. I was assisted in my need to avoid this desire by life's practicalities. There was the need to make a living, and I could always give myself entirely over to whatever job I held so that there was nothing left at the end of the day for writing. There was the need to complete graduate school assignments, and these had a way of expanding to take up whatever life space was available to them and then some. And then there was the inexorability and "alwaysness" of caring for children. Children, in fact, are the perfect excuse for avoiding the creative demands of the soul.

When I was a child, my mother was very interested in theater. She volunteered for a local theater company, saw as many productions as she could, and read and reread the great playwrights. Eventually she began writing plays of her own, commuting into New York once a week to take classes. She received encouraging feedback but finally put the drafts in a drawer and her dreams on the shelf. She told herself—and us—that she couldn't pursue being a playwright because being a mother came first.

"We each have an appointment with ourselves," writes Jungian analyst Jim Hollis, "though most of us never show up for it."[3] I have empathy for my mother and her need to use her children as an excuse to avoid her appointment with herself. She came from an era and a life situation that made pushing through her fears and self-doubts extraordinarily difficult. My path has been easier, and yet I have had to contend with the legacy of my mother's struggle. When my children were young, I was plagued by a fear that I couldn't both care for them in the way I wanted to and realize my creative potential. Even though my life was very different from my mother's, there was a persistent undertow that convinced me a tragic sacrifice might somehow be inevitable. It took conscious work to undo that knot. I had to create an image of the life I wanted—a life that included abundant warm connection with my children as well as meaningful work and creative pursuits.

SHARPENING OUR FOCUS

By the time I had finished training, my children were still quite young, and I had a practice that was quickly growing. My desire to write had not diminished, however. The pressure that this desire exerted on my psyche caused me considerable unhappiness, but it also demanded that I focus on what mattered to me. I had to admit to myself that if writing were important—and I knew that it was—it was up to me to make room for it. It wouldn't do to use my children as an excuse for not creating. The competing requirements of motherhood, work, and the creative demands of the soul invited me to become ruthless with how I spent my time—not a bad thing! I quit knitting. Gardening likewise fell by the wayside. I spent time only with friends who mattered. I gave up following television shows I had never really liked. I permitted myself not to feel obligated to throw elaborate dinner parties. I spent most of every day caring for and being with my children, but I let go of any expectations of myself that didn't fit with my deeply held goals.

In a sense, the significant demands on my time as a result of being a mother *forced* me to claim my creative desires and to take them seriously. There was no other way to proceed. Total commitment to writing was the only alternative to abandoning my ambition altogether. As a result, my focus sharpened. I hungrily grasped whatever scraps of time were available. For several years, my writing time was during my son's weekly chess lesson, but in part due to this, I made sure that I wrote at least once per week.

Barbara Kingsolver notes how being a mother sharpened her focus and required her to use her time as efficiently as possible. She contrasts her writing rituals with those of writers without children.

> My jaw drops when I hear of the rituals some authors use to put themselves in the so-called mood to write . . . Diane Ackerman begins each summer day "by choosing and arranging flowers for a Zenlike hour or so." She listens to music obsessively, then speed-walks for an hour, every single day. "I don't know whether this helps or not," she allows, in *A Natural History of the Senses*. "My muse is male, has the radiant, silvery complexion of the moon, and never speaks to me directly."
>
> My muse wears a baseball cap, backward. The minute my daughter is on the school bus, he saunters up behind me with a bat slung over his shoulder and says oh so directly, "Okay, author lady, you've got six hours till that bus rolls back up the drive. You can sit down and write, *now*, or you can think about looking for a day job."[4]

The exigencies of raising children can force us to concentrate with a laser-like focus on our priorities. We may come to tend our creative offspring with as much protective ferocity as our biological offspring, fighting to claim both against other demands. A well-loved fairy tale addresses this theme.

RUMPELSTILTSKIN

A poor miller had a beautiful daughter. He happened one day to meet the king, and to make himself appear interesting and important, he told the king that his daughter could spin straw into gold. The king was quite taken by this and commanded that the miller's daughter be brought to the palace that same day.

When the miller's daughter arrived at the palace, the king led her to a room filled with straw. In the middle of it sat a spinning wheel. "Get to work," he told her. "If you don't manage to spin all of this straw into gold by morning, you shall die." With that, he left and closed the door.

The poor miller's daughter didn't know what to do. She hadn't any idea how to spin straw into gold. At last, she sat down and began to cry. At that moment, a tiny man appeared. "Why are you weeping so, miller-maid?" he asked. The miller's daughter explained her predicament. "What will you give me if I spin for you?" he asked. "My necklace," she replied. He nodded. She handed him her necklace, and he set to work. One by one, he filled the bobbins with lustrous gold, and when the morning came, the king was astonished and delighted to find the miller's daughter alone, sleeping among the piles of golden thread.

That evening, however, he led her to a much bigger room filled with even more straw than the night before. Once again, he commanded her to spin or forfeit her life. As on the previous night, the miller's daughter dissolved into tears, after which the little man reappeared and asked what the matter was. "What will you give me if I spin for you?" he asked. "My ring," she replied. And once the trade was made, the little man set to work as he had the night before.

Once again, the king was delighted in the morning, but was hungry only for more gold and set the miller's daughter an even greater quantity of straw to spin the following night. However, he promised that if she could spin for the third time, he would marry her.

This time, when the little man asked what she would give him, the miller's daughter replied that she had nothing more to offer. "Then promise me your firstborn child," said the little man. The miller's daughter gasped, but thought to herself, *Who knows if that will ever happen?* And so she agreed. As before, the little man worked quickly to fill all of the bobbins with gold thread. The next morning, the king was as delighted as ever and wedding preparations began.

One year later, the new queen gave birth to a son. She had completely forgotten about the little man, until one day he appeared and demanded what had been promised him. Stricken, the queen begged and pleaded to be allowed to keep her baby. The little man took pity on her. "I will give you three days. If you can guess my name in that amount of time, you may keep your child."

The queen spent the following night making a list of all manner of names. When the little man appeared that morning, she tried them all, but he simply answered, "That is not my name" to each guess. The second day proceeded much the same. On the evening of the third day, the queen sent her faithful female companion to discover any new names. The woman returned with a strange story: amid the forest she had seen a little man hopping around a fire and singing

> To-morrow I brew, to-day I bake,
> And then the child away I'll take;
> For little deems my royal dame
> That Rumpelstiltskin is my name!

Of course, the queen was delighted to hear this. When the little man returned on the third day, the queen guessed that his name was Rumpelstiltskin, whereupon the little man tore himself in two in a rage and was never heard from again.

The poor miller uses his beautiful daughter to enhance his sense of importance, and in doing so, he places her in mortal peril. It is a story, then, about a wound caused by the father—a father wound—and its effects on the psyche of the daughter. In my work with women, I have seen again and again that a father wound can inhibit a woman's ability to inhabit her creative potential.

DEMONIC CREATIVITY

If we showed a creative promise as a child but had a parent who traded on our abilities, we may have become divorced from our talents. A child in such a position may feel extreme pressure to perform. If the child comes to believe that parental love and approval rest on achievement, she may feel driven to perfectionism. Her creative pursuits become a never-ending quest to achieve. They take on a pressured, unhappy quality rather than being undertaken in a spirit of playfulness or joy. It is as if the creative ability no longer rests in the child but belongs in some way to the parent. In this way, creativity can begin to feel *daimonic*.

The word *daimon* comes from the Greek word for demon, referring to a transpersonal force that drives humans forward toward either self-destruction or self-actualization. It is associated with the idea of a fiend, but also with the autonomous spirit of genius that motivates and inspires great artistic endeavors. In Plato's *Republic*, he recounts the Myth of Er, which tells how each human soul is assigned a unique daimon before we are born. This daimon selects an image or pattern that is ours to live out throughout our life. Though we forget this calling, our daimon remembers. Therefore, the daimon acts as the bearer of our destiny.

Rumpelstiltskin is just such a fiendish creative daimon—or demon. He seems to "remember" the tremendous talents that the miller's daughter possesses that she doesn't know she has. He is capable of performing amazing feats of creative genius, but at the same time, he torments the soul whom he serves. Researchers looking at motivation and passion may have articulated an aspect of daimonic creativity. The social psychologist Robert Vallerand and colleagues at the University of Quebec at Montreal surveyed college students about their preferred activities. From this data set, they were able to form a distinction between what they termed a "harmonious passion" versus an "obsessive passion."[5] With an obsessive passion, the person has lost control of how she engages in that activity. She pursues it in a pressured way, seeking self-esteem or social acceptance. Sometimes, she pursues a passion as a result of an uncontrollable urge. She may find that her sense of self has become dependent on her passion. In a sense, her creative endeavor has become a kind of addiction. This is indeed a description of daimonic creativity.

The miller's beautiful daughter is not in touch with her creative potential. It appears to exist entirely outside of her, and she can perform only at the demand and for the benefit of others. Rumpelstiltskin is a personification of her split-off creativity. He's a morally ambivalent little demon who appears at the right moment to save her when she sinks into tears but threatens to take everything from her. Engaging in her creative endeavor leaves her depleted and others enriched—she must give up what little she has and even promise her unborn child while she makes the king wealthy.

The image of spinning straw into gold must be one of the loveliest, most poetic metaphors in the world of fairy tales. It suggests the subtle art of the alchemists who sought to transform something base and common into gold. Straw is a by-product of grain production, left over after the grain and chaff have been removed. It is useful only as bedding or stuffing. Creative endeavors can have a similar quality. Using just our imagination, some paper, and a pen, a writer spins a story, perhaps creating something of lasting value.

We might imagine that the miller's daughter has a tremendous creative talent that she is unable to access in an unconflicted way due to her father wound. When pressured to perform for someone else's benefit, she can do so but is left feeling drained and impoverished as a result. Her abilities allow her to experience a provisional success, but a threat menaces her. However, once she has a baby, the miller's daughter is no longer content to be a passive victim to her daimonic creative urges. When her child is it stake, she becomes able to take her relationship with her creativity in hand.

It is a widespread belief throughout many cultures that knowing the true name of something gives you power over it. Naming a problem has the effect of pinning it down and defining it, thereby rendering it easier to address. When we are struggling with an inner problem, putting it into words can give us power over it. When the queen learns Rumpelstiltskin's name, she has gained mastery over him and he can no longer torment her. We might imagine that, psychologically, this part of the tale indicates that she has been able to reclaim her creative genius, integrating it so that it is now at her conscious disposal rather than seeming to exist outside her or for others' benefit. In the case of the miller's daughter, her creative daimon comes to her when she is in despair—otherwise, she cannot access it. It isn't until her child is threatened that she finds the fortitude and means to *integrate* this creative potential. By naming it, she reclaims it.

PARENTAL NARCISSISM

Corinne was an extraordinarily talented and dynamic woman who had had a successful career in marketing before going on maternity leave. She recalls a distant relationship with her father, whom she often experienced as cold, rejecting, and critical. As a child, she was an avid reader who liked to write stories. She remembers that when adults would ask her what she wanted to be when she grew up, she would say she wanted to be an author. This was likely to bring on a bit of a lecture by her father, who would warn her that "writers didn't make any money."

Corinne was academically gifted and did very well in school. This pleased her father, but Corinne recalls that his approval felt tentative, as though it would last only until the next quiz or test. Corinne told me that her father was often distant and short-tempered when she was in high school. When she received a report card of all As, however, he would become jovial and solicitous toward her for a few days before retreating again into irritability. She and I remarked together on how this experience matched the feeling in the fairy tale "Rumpelstiltskin"—once one room was spun, there was just a larger room waiting for her.

She also felt that her father claimed her talents for his purposes. When she won a statewide writing competition in high school, she was thrilled to have her literary talent acknowledged. Her father focused on an entirely different aspect of the achievement, announcing to the family that, when Corinne competed at something, she always won. By framing her accomplishment in terms that cast Corinne as successful in a way that he valued, he was trading on her achievements for his own gain—a little like the miller bragging to the king.

The effect of this paternal narcissism on Corinne was far-reaching. She entered adulthood lacking confidence in her abilities and unable to get anywhere near her deeply held desire to become a writer. By the time Corinne became a mother, she was in the midst of a successful career in marketing—a field related to that of her father. In effect, her ability to spin straw into academic gold had led her into a conventionally successful career, like the miller's daughter marrying the king. She had initially intended to take three months off for maternity leave before returning to work, but she found herself rethinking that decision shortly after her daughter arrived.

Corinne wound up quitting her job to stay home with her child. With the birth of her baby, she had a real sense of clarity that it wasn't going to be worth leaving her daughter to do just anything. Her whole sense of her priorities shifted, and it became apparent to her that she needed to put her offspring—biological as well as creative—first. Within a few years, Corinne started a graduate writing program at a nearby university, in part as a way to enforce some fenced-off time for writing. She eventually went on to become a writer and writing teacher full time, publishing several well-received novels. Like the miller's daughter, Corinne's commitment to her biological child helped her find her commitment to her creative child.

Thus, while it is undoubtedly true that mothering presents significant challenges to a woman's ability to live out her creativity, there are ways in which it can kindle a more substantial commitment to her creative process. For novelist Fay Weldon, having children connected her with her creative fertility.

Another thing that seems quite helpful to the creative process is having babies. It does not detract at all from one's creativity. It reminds one that there is always more where that came from and there is never any shortage of ideas or the ability to create. The process of being pregnant and then of having the baby and getting up in the night only puts one more in touch with this fecund part of one's self.[6]

STRAW INTO GOLD

Like the miller's daughter and Corinne, Harry Potter creator J.K. Rowling describes what very much sounds like a father wound. According to a 2012 interview in *The New Yorker*, Rowling has said that her father frightened her. "I did not have an easy relationship with my father," she told the interviewer, admitting that she hadn't had contact with him at that point in nine years.

She said that the break had already happened when, in December, 2003, Peter Rowling offered his Harry Potter first editions for sale, at Sotheby's; some of them did not sell, but others did, including a copy of "Harry Potter and the Goblet of Fire," given to him on Father's Day, 2000, and signed, "Lots of love from your first born," with a drawing of a hand reaching for a running gnome. It went for forty-eight thousand dollars.[7]

Although we don't know much about the nature of Rowling's relationship with his daughter, we can see in his profitable sale of his daughter's books a tendency to trade on her talent for his gain, much like the miller in our fairy tale.

And, of course, Rowling was able to turn straw into literary gold, spinning a tale from her imagination that has enchanted millions. Rowling has stated that the story about the boy wizard first presented itself to her while she was on a train when she was twenty-five, and she began writing it down almost immediately. Shortly after, she moved to Portugal to teach English. She taught in the evenings and wrote during the day. She also met and married a local journalist named Jorge Arantes.

Rowling's marriage was reportedly stormy and challenging from the start. As discussed in *The New Yorker* interview and in biographies of the author, Arantes was frequently jealous, and there were noisy rows. When Rowling became pregnant, the couple moved into Arantes's mother's small apartment, and it was while living here that Rowling became a mother in the summer of 1993. Her marriage ended soon after when the relationship turned violent. After a heated argument during which Arantes dragged her out of the house and slapped her, Rowling fled from Portugal with minimal belongings, her baby daughter—and the first three chapters of *Harry Potter and the Philosopher's Stone*.

The next phase of Rowling's life has become legendary. Living on welfare in Edinburgh in a mouse-infested apartment, Rowling undertook the long, arduous journey toward building a life for herself and her child. In the midst of this, she continued to write. She would take her daughter on walks in the stroller, and when the baby fell asleep, Rowling would stop into a coffee shop and write. Rowling credits her daughter for giving her the focus to finish the book.

> I was trying to write through that time, and I did. But it
> was patchy and fitful and sometimes I just didn't have the focus
> to do it. . . . Having that child forced me to finish the bloody
> book. Not because I thought it was going to save us but because
> I thought it was going to be my last chance to finish it.[8]

Having to care for her daughter forced Rowling to take herself and her creative work more seriously—she realized she needed to show up for that appointment with herself.

Mothering can support a woman's creative work in other ways as well. Being a mother can invite us to trust our instincts, perhaps for the first time. This can give us confidence, allowing us to stretch into our creative capacity. One woman with whom I worked commented that mothering gave her confidence for the first time in her life because she could see that what she did by instinct worked.

A Scottish fairy tale provides an image of how mothering can teach us to trust our inner resources.

THE STOLEN BAIRN AND THE SIDH

Once upon a time, a young mother was walking along a seaside path with her baby in her arms when he began to cry. Knowing he was thirsty, she set him down carefully in the soft grass so that she could draw up water from a nearby stream. However, the moment she left, two women of the Sidh, powerful fairies, came along and took the bairn (child).

When the mother returned to find her child gone, she cried out and began searching in desperation. She walked and walked until she reached a nearby village, and she asked everyone she saw if they had seen her bairn. But they could tell her nothing.

At last, she came to a gypsy camp. Here, she sought out the wisdom of the gypsy grandmother, who was said to possess great wisdom. The gypsy grandmother advised the young woman to give up the search for the child. She said he had been stolen by the Sidh and taken to their secret kingdom beneath the earth. She advised that any mortal who went there could never leave. But the young mother was undeterred. She begged the gypsy grandmother to help her find a way to rescue her child.

The gypsy grandmother told the young woman that the day was coming when the Sidh would be choosing a new ruler. If the mother could find a way into their secret kingdom at this time, there might be a way she could win back her child. The gypsy grandmother went on to tell her that the Sidh had no power to make anything of their own and therefore they always had to beg or steal. They were very vain and always interested in possessing things that had no equal anywhere. If the mother could obtain some rich and rare items, she might be able to convince the Sidh to return her child.

"But how can a poor lass such as I find something that is rich and rare beyond compare?" the young woman asked. The gypsy grandmother had no answer but gave the woman her blessing.

The young mother once again despaired, for she was poor and had no means to buy fine and rare things. Not knowing what else to do, she made her way to the sea. There, she gathered down from eider ducks. When she had enough, she wove a gown as soft and white as a cloud with a border of golden flowers.

Next, she found animal bones on the beach that had been bleached and smoothed by the tide until they were as white as ivory. From these, she fashioned a harp and strung it with strings of her own golden hair. When she played it, the music was so sweet that the birds gathered round. "Now I am ready," she said.

She donned her white gown with the golden border and took up her white harp with its golden strings. Then she went to find the entrance to the fairy kingdom and waited.

The day had come for the Sidh to choose their new ruler, and as they were gathering at the entrance to their secret kingdom, one of them spotted the young woman in her beautiful eiderdown cloak. "What will you take for your cloak?" the Sidh asked her. "You can have as much gold as you like!" The woman told the fairy that she would give her the cloak in exchange for being admitted to the secret fairy kingdom and given an audience with the king. The trade was made, and the Sidh took her by the hand into the underground world of the fairies and led her to the king.

The mother sat down before the king of Sidh and took out her harp that she had strung with her own hair. The Sidh were so entranced by the beauty of the music that they begged her to give it to them. "It has a price," she responded. The Sidh assured her she could have whatever she wanted.

"My bairn, and nothing else!" So the Sidh gave her back her child, and while they were marveling over the harp and the beauty of its music, she took her child in her arms and slipped out of the fairy kingdom and didn't stop until she was back safe at home with her bairn.

Like the child of the miller's daughter in "Rumpelstiltskin," the bairn in this story is endangered by a daimonic force that wishes to claim the child for its own. We know little about this young woman other than that she has access to few resources. When we have limited access to our psychic assets, we may have difficulty trusting our creative instincts or claiming our desire to be creative. When this is the case, our creative children can indeed be easily taken from us.

TRUSTING OURSELVES

The young mother in the story needs to find rich and rare things, but at first despairs that she will be able to do so since she is just a poor lass. Psychologically, this would be a situation in which we have trouble believing in our creative abilities. Perhaps we assume that we aren't talented enough to warrant pursuing our artistic interests seriously, for example. The mother in the story must push through her self-doubt if she is to rescue her child. It may be that, like J. K. Rowling, we don't fully commit ourselves to our creative life until our children somehow make doing so an urgent proposition.

Despite her poverty and the doubt she feels that she will ever find anything good enough, the materials the young mother needs are readily available from her environment. And it is the case that when we face a trial or crisis, this is often the moment when we become acquainted with the resources—both inner and outer—that have perhaps been there all along, though we did not realize it.

Most poignant of all is that the harp is strung with the mother's hair. Often, the thing that our children—creative and actual—need most is *us*, even with all our flaws and imperfections. Bringing ourselves to our relationship with our children and our creative endeavors is often just what is needed.

The ordinary nature of the fine and precious things the heroine finds underscores an important point about creative life. While you may associate creativity with writers, painters, poets, and dancers, the urge to inhabit a new attitude, to take a fresh look at an old problem, or to dream up a new orientation to life are all examples of the soul's irrepressible creative instinct. We are all artists at heart. The word *create* comes from an older word that implied a sense of making something out of nothing. When we are creative, we bring something into the world that wasn't there before. If you are a mother who has not found your creative medium, look to where the energy is. What draws you? What fills you with excitement? It might be planning the next family vacation, cooking a delicious meal, or coming up with a novel solution to a problem. All of these are ways in which our creative instincts find expression. We should tend these fires wherever they burn.

My client Aurora grew up with a depressed and distant mother and an alcoholic father. When she was quite young, her parents divorced. Aurora was an intuitive child whose naturally fiery temperament had to go underground for her to accommodate herself to her father's absence due to alcohol and her mother's absence due to depression. She, therefore, made it to adulthood before she had ever authentically entertained the question of what she truly wanted from life.

Vocation was an area that Aurora and I explored in our work together. Though she had a job that was sometimes engaging, she also felt that she hadn't found the right place to use her many gifts and talents. When she became pregnant with her second child, issues around career came into heightened focus. She questioned whether she wanted to go back to work after maternity leave, and she allowed herself to ponder a future career change. After her son's birth, she felt a renewed sense of confidence as she faced these tough questions. Mothering this second baby helped her to feel more competent and powerful generally, and this sense carried over into her vocational and creative pursuits. When the baby was several months old, she had the following dream.

> I had a baby, and I was pumping breast milk. The baby was there, but he was being cared for by another woman because I had given him up for adoption. I was filling bottles and bottles with breast milk. It was like a gallon! I realized that the baby was my son, and I wanted him back. I got angry that the other woman had my son. I told her that she had two choices: she could move closer to me, or she could give me my son back. I was

worried that they were going to retaliate and keep my son. I left
and went outside. These ninjas came to train me. I came back
stronger. I thought that now I could be a good politician.

Like the mother in the fairy tale, Aurora was susceptible to giving away her precious creative children because of how she had been unmothered in her childhood. She had seldom allowed herself to entertain ambitious dreams for her professional future. When ideas did present themselves, she would usually shoot them down as impractical or out of her reach. Similarly, the mother in the fairy tale quickly loses track of her baby. He is easily stolen away from her.

In the dream, Aurora had given away her son, just as she can so easily give away her dreams for herself. And yet, just like the mother in the story, Aurora was surprised to realize that she had amazing inner resources at her disposal that she hadn't known about before. She produced prodigious amounts of milk for her baby, and she was trained to be a strong, elite fighter. This gives her the ability to be a good politician. A politician is someone who has access to power and uses it, hopefully, in the interest of serving others. In the dream, Aurora seems to find access to these resources and strengths as she is seeking to get back her child, much as happens for the mother in the fairy tale.

In her outer life, the birth of her son helped Aurora permit herself to envision creative possibilities for her future. She was able to do a better job of tending to the offspring of her imagination. In so doing, she gained surprising access to as yet unrealized aspects of herself. She discovered that she had renewed energy for her current job, where she stretched into additional roles with new-found confidence. In addition, she became interested in exploring heretofore unacknowledged talents, wondering whether she might want to start her own business one day.

Children have a way of demanding everything from us. Especially when our children are young, merely getting through the day can leave us depleted and exhausted, with little time for anything else. A woman's creative life can readily become mired beneath the daily duties of motherhood. And yet motherhood can be an invitation to commit ourselves more deeply to our artistic offspring, offering renewed opportunities to trust in our creative potential. Motherhood, with its call to embodiment and authenticity, can provide a deep grounding for meaningful creative endeavors.

Questions for Reflection for Claiming Creativity

1. How did creativity show up in your life before having kids? How has it shown up since you became a mother? What have been the difficulties in holding on to a creative practice or expression while parenting? How has motherhood enriched your creative life?

2. The miller trades on his daughter's alleged talents by bragging about her, and this results in her being given to the king who likewise treats her as if her talents are purely for his own enrichment. If we have a father wound, this can affect our connection with our creativity and influence the kind of relationships we choose. What was your relationship like with your father? How has it supported or hampered your relationship with your creativity?

3. In essence, the miller gives away his daughter to the king. Later, the miller's daughter promises to give away her first child to Rumpelstiltskin. The way we were parented can have a profound effect on how we later parent. In what ways has your relationship with your father impacted your parenting?

4. The miller's daughter promises her child to Rumpelstiltskin, while the young mother in "The Stolen Bairn and the Sidh" loses her baby when she sets him down for a minute. How have you lost or promised away your precious creative offspring?

5. The miller's daughter must gain power over the daimonic force that controls her creativity if she is to save her child. How has motherhood helped you to sharpen your focus on your creative goals?

6. The mother in "The Stolen Bairn and the Sidh" has few resources and, at first, must manage the crisis on her own. At last, she is able to turn to the gypsy grandmother, an image of an inner feminine content that has been devalued or marginalized. If you have faced a crisis while mothering either your actual children or your creative offspring, where have you turned? What inner or outer resources have you discovered?

7. The young mother in "The Stolen Bairn and the Sidh" discovers her tremendous creative potential when she must look within in order to rescue her son. Sometimes facing a challenge is what shows us that we are capable of more than we knew. How has motherhood helped you to see your creative strengths in ways you may not have appreciated before?

CHAPTER 9

Claiming Authority

Most of our difficulties come from losing
contact with our instincts, with the age-
old forgotten wisdom stored up in us.

C. G. JUNG
IN C. G. JUNG SPEAKING

At the end of "The Two Caskets," the heroine is gifted with gold and jewels upon her successful return from the bottom of the well. Gold and jewels are richly symbolic because of their beauty and permanence. Gold does not tarnish or dim. Precious stones do not rot or wilt. The benefits of the psychological work we have been exploring in this book are of an enduring nature. Becoming attuned to our instinctual wisdom so that we can stand in our inner authority is one of those benefits.

Most of us in our culture are severed to an extent from our instinctual wisdom. In the process of growing up, we are necessarily taught to disconnect ourselves from those natural promptings that bubble up from our depths. We're taught to divorce ourselves from anger and aggression, to ignore subtle fears, and to push away desire so that we can meet the expectations of the culture. We lose touch with how it feels to be in our bodies. We may find it challenging to listen to the subtle cues from deep within that let us know what we are feeling, what we need, or when we are sensing a bat squeak of danger. We forget how to listen to the whispers of the soul, and we shut down our most tender yearnings.

INSTINCT

Since our instincts generally point us in the direction we must go if we are to follow the path of individuation, being cut off from them can leave us adrift amid our life, unsure of where we are going or how to proceed. Reconnecting with our instincts invites us to accept responsibility for our lives and to claim our inner authority. *Authority* comes from the Latin word *auctor*, which means "master," "leader," or "author." When we claim our authority, we become the authors of our lives and the masters of our fate.

Motherhood offers us the opportunity to connect with the unconscious wisdom of instinct, for we realize early on that our children's well-being depends on our ability to hear and trust these inner promptings. If we cannot do so, we—and our children—suffer. When we are unmoored from our instinctual foundations, mothering can be particularly difficult. Growing up in a culture that places such a high value on rationality, we may silence voices that warn us of dangers, or we may cruelly reject our irrational yearnings. The English fairy tale "The Hobyahs" illustrates this tendency to destroy our instincts and shows its effect on our psyches and those of our children.

THE HOBYAHS

Once there was a little girl who lived with an old man and woman in a house made of hemp stalks. They had a little dog named Turpie. One night, the terrible Hobyahs came and said, "Hobyah! Hobyah! Hobyah! Tear down the hemp stalks, eat up the old man and woman, and carry off the little girl!" But Turpie barked and scared the Hobyahs away. The old man, however, was angry because the barking had awakened him. In the morning, he cut off the dog's tail.

The next night, the Hobyahs came again and said, "Hobyah! Hobyah! Hobyah! Tear down the hemp stalks, eat up the old man and woman, and carry off the little girl!" But Turpie barked again, scaring off the Hobyahs and saving the family. The old man was angry once again because the barking woke him up. In the morning, he cut off one of Turpie's legs.

The following night, everything happened as before. Once again, in the morning, the old man cut off another one of Turpie's legs. Things continued in this fashion until Turpie had no more legs. Still he barked at night when the Hobyahs came, so in the morning, the old man cut off his head.

The next night the Hobyahs came again and said "Hobyah! Hobyah! Hobyah! Tear down the hemp stalks, eat up the old man and woman, and carry off the little girl!" And when the Hobyahs found that little dog Turpie's head was off, they tore down hemp stalks, ate up the old man and old woman, and carried off the little girl in a bag.

The Hobyahs took the little girl back to their home, hung up the bag, and went to sleep, for Hobyahs sleep during the daytime. The little girl cried so loudly that a man with a big dog passing by heard her. He rescued her from the bag and put the dog in her place.

When the Hobyahs took the bag down that night and opened it, the big dog jumped out and ate them all up, so there are no Hobyahs now.

Turpie represents our helpful instincts, which will always be there to guide us, even when we refuse to listen to them. Turpie movingly does not cease his barking no matter how he is disregarded and maimed. So too, our dreams—carriers of unconscious wisdom—continue to visit us whether or not we pay attention to them. The old man who effects these punishments on the dog could be understood as an internalized voice of that aspect of our culture or family that dismisses our fears or tells us we are crazy for having our feelings. He would like to stay asleep—that is, unconscious—to the danger that visits them.

Interestingly, the old woman in the story is only briefly mentioned. Her voice is silenced to such an extent that she is incapable of standing up to the old man and protecting the child. Eventually, when Turpie has been killed, the destructive Hobyahs devour both the old man and woman, leaving the child unprotected.

When we disregard our inner promptings in favor of advice from "experts," we amputate and maim our instincts. In the following passage, a mother grieves for the way she allowed her instincts to be silenced and her inner Turpie to be dismembered.

I am wheeled into the labor room. It is the early 60s and consciousness is out . . . being unconscious is in, and I am given an injection to create twilight sleep. In the delivery room I feel nothing, I see nothing. My only recall is of someone shaking my arm and I vaguely hear, "You have a boy." It is the early 60s, and I never get to see my son until many hours after the birth. It is the early 60s and rooming in (mother and child) is not permitted in hospitals. Fathers can only visit during hours. Breastfeeding is out . . . formula is in . . . having a nurse for four weeks is in . . . bonding with the baby is . . . well, no one really even talks about the bonding process.

My husband and I may be parents, but we are still kids ourselves. . . . When the nurse leaves after four weeks, I begin to cry. The impact hits hard. At twenty-three, I am tied down. I am on a schedule of feeding, changing, bathing, sleeping. I am ripe for the advice that I hear . . . "Don't spoil him . . . don't pick him up . . . let him cry. That's what we did with you. Listen to us . . . we are your parents and after raising two children, we know what is right. The worst thing is to give in when he cries . . . Oh, you can see if he needs to be changed or fed, but if he doesn't need that, then let him cry and eventually he'll go to sleep."

I buy their ádvice . . . I want to be a good mother and have an unspoiled child, and so I feed, I diaper, I bathe, and when I hear the crying, I let him cry.

At some time during the early 80s, I begin to notice women breastfeeding their babies in public places and in the quiet confines of their homes. On the Oprah show I learn that having wants and needs are OK. I am hearing words like "contact" and "warmth" and the "bonding process." Something in me is painfully sad. Something in me is

wanting to cry. I long to return to my infant son and pick
him up and kiss his baby tears; I yearn to cuddle him and
coo him to sleep, but having that second chance is out.

It is the 90s . . . my son is a grown man and for me,
feeling the pain and the feelings is in.[1]

The author's repetition of the decade helps reminds us of the extent
to which our ability to attend to our inner knowing is informed by the
cultural context in which we find ourselves. Contemporary American
women often enter motherhood without access to traditional knowledge that has been passed down from one woman to another. Therefore,
we become susceptible to whichever expert voice happens to hold sway
in the culture at a given time. Changes in breastfeeding illustrate how
a cultural norm can ravage our instinctual response. Nursing is a biological behavior several million years old that, along with intercourse,
has ensured the survival and propagation of our species. Yet, within
a scant forty years in the middle of the twentieth century, it was very
nearly eliminated in the industrial world.

In her memoir of motherhood, *What I Thought I Knew*, Alice Eve
Cohen tells a chilling tale of wounded feminine instincts. Having been
told she was infertile due to her mother having taken DES—or dieth-
ylstilbestrol, the first synthetic estrogen—the author and her doctor
misdiagnose the author's pregnancy symptoms. Her missed periods
and upset stomach are attributed to menopause. For her painful
breasts, swollen abdomen, and inability to sleep, she is subjected to
x-rays and prescribed high doses of synthetic estrogen. When she seeks
medical advice due to concern that the frightening bulge in her stomach is a tumor, she undergoes an emergency CAT scan, which finds
that the tumor is a second-trimester fetus. The hormones to which she
was exposed during pregnancy affected the development of the baby
so that it had ambiguous genitalia in utero.

Cohen's story is a very personal example of how the feminine is
wounded by our divorce from our instincts. Her fertility is damaged by the prescriptions of the medical establishment that gave
her mother DES. The same medical establishment supports her

in denying her bodily reality. In spite of symptoms of exhaustion, nausea, anemia, frequent need to urinate, sore breasts, sore hip joints, and reflux, neither she nor her physician suspects pregnancy. At one point after the pregnancy is discovered, a doctor with whom she consults about a possible abortion tells her pointedly, "You're also an idiot! You were in denial for the past six months. Every woman knows subliminally when she's pregnant."[2] It is symbolically fitting that the child she carries is a girl with ambiguous genitalia. Happily, Cohen's daughter is born essentially healthy.

MEETING THE DARK FEMININE

We desperately need our feminine instincts when we mother, and these may be imaged in dreams and fairy tales by an old woman. Luckily, pregnancy and motherhood invite us into contact with our instinctual wisdom. The body, especially the female body, is the province of the dark feminine, which was banished long ago in our culture. We learn our bodies are shameful, dirty, dangerous, or lusty. We become split off from them, unable to listen to their wisdom. We abhor them for being the wrong size, or shape, or color. Western women are bound to be cut off from our bodies to a greater or lesser degree. Pregnancy, childbirth, nursing, and caring for small children are fundamentally physical, embodied experiences. Pregnancy is a time when a woman is often confronted with her physicality. One woman was repeatedly visited by the archetypal old woman of the body during her first pregnancy via the following dream.

> *I am pulling up potato plants from a field. An old, unknown*
> *woman comes up to me. Then I see that the potatoes are really*
> *nice little dolls in the earth. The old woman tells me that the*
> *dolls are my fetus. I am amazed and become filled with mixed*
> *emotions. Finally, I wake up very upset.*[3]

The dreamer is being initiated into the secrets of gestation and birth. The old woman is a kind of Great Mother goddess who lets her know that what she is going through is not under ego control but part of the great mystery of life and death.

During pregnancy, our bodily reality overtakes us in the form of exhaustion and nausea. We cannot will away the backaches or leg cramps. We cannot ignore our swelling belly. And, of course, we cannot ignore the sheer primal physicality of labor and childbirth. When we go home with our new baby, we find ourselves firmly in the realm of the body, dealing with feces, spit-up, pee, blood, and breast milk on an hourly basis. For what may be the first time, we completely tune in to subtle physical processes, monitoring our newborn's breathing, the fluttering eyelids that denote sleepiness, the quiet fussiness that lets us know he is hungry before he starts to cry. Throughout pregnancy and nursing, we may learn a new appreciation for the silent, mysterious wisdom of our bodies that knows how to knit up a whole new person from two tiny cells and how to create food to feed him. I remember being awestruck that my milk would let down whenever my baby cried.

Both instinctual, bodily wisdom and the fiery emotions that would allow us to act on this wisdom even against the wishes of the dominant culture are qualities of the archetypal old woman who is part of the feminine shadow. An encounter with her—with our angry, authentic, witchy bitch—can reconnect us with her power. When we become mothers, we may seek out the old woman because we know she has some wisdom we desperately need. When her first child, Benjamin, was a baby, author and memoirist Jane Lazarre found herself dreaming of hidden rooms in her apartment.

> *I walk into the unused apartment behind the one I am living in. Shocked, I discover that people are living there. . . .*
>
> *I dream that I let him cry too long. When I finally go to get him, he is sick and bleeding from too much crying. He is naked and has lost a lot of weight. He has lost his beautiful curly hair.*
>
> *Clutching him, I run to the people who live in the back rooms. I tell them to call a doctor. When they leave to make*

the call, I notice they have decorated the apartment beautifully.
Everything is clean. The couch is golden brocade. Then I notice
that this is only one of the unused apartments. Behind it is
another. I walk in, still carrying Benjamin, and see that it is not
kept well. It looks like a furnished room, without personality or
character. I am surprised that I have such easy access to these two
apartments. But there is a third one which I have never entered.
It is dark. I feel there is someone there who can make Benjamin
well, perhaps my grandmother who died when I was a girl. I
cover him with one of his old baby blankets, hold him close,
looking at the dark room.[4]

In the dream, Lazarre knows that she must go toward the darkness where the archetypal old woman lives. There she would find the wisdom she needs to mother her son.

SILENCING AN INNER KNOWING

By the time I reached adulthood, I had been well schooled in questioning my instincts. When I became a mother at thirty-six, I was old enough to have begun reclaiming some of my lost instinctual wisdom. But my instinctual mode of mothering constantly seemed under attack, and tragically, I have not always been able to withstand the challenge.

When my son was two months old, we bid on a new house. I was ambivalent about it but felt overwhelmed with the new baby and awash in postpartum hormones. Around that same time, I read an article in a parenting magazine about a child who had gotten lead poisoning, and some mysterious internal warning bells went off. I saved the article. I vowed we would get the house tested once we moved. But after the move, money was tight. I continued to worry about lead. I woke up one morning terrified, suddenly having put it together that the previous owner had made stained glass in the room that was now my playroom. Didn't stained glass use lead? I made an appointment to discuss this with my pediatrician. He told me I was right to be concerned, that we should have the children tested, and that if they tested normal, I should feel "reassured." Both children had blood lead levels of four, well within the normal range.

But I continued to worry. My fears about a toxin in the house surrounded me like a vapor. They were seemingly irrational, and yet somehow I could not get them out of my mind. Were my worries coming from a deep instinctual place? Or was it merely anxiety speaking? Discerning a deep knowing from a more superficial prompting can be difficult to do, especially when you have been instructed by the culture and perhaps also by your family of origin to disregard instinct and intuition. Instinct speaks to you when you are still. Anxiety gnaws at you when your mind is uneasy. Anxiety is often confused with intuition, but when a true intuition makes itself known, you recognize it as something quite distinct. It speaks in a soft, vague whisper and yet it has a knowing at its heart. What we need to discern one thing from another is trust—trust in ourselves, our bodies, and our process. Like the little dog Turpie, an instinct doesn't stop warning us even when we disregard it.

My intuition about a potential danger to my son would not leave me alone, even though I only put tentative trust in it. The idea of the lead that might be in our house haunted me. I asked all the neighbors of their experiences and got vague but reassuring answers. Just don't do any remodeling work without having the surfaces involved tested, they told me. When the local painters dropped off their business card, I saved it, hoping we might paint some areas that were chipping. I bought special cleaners and tried my best to mop the floors as often as possible. At every doctor's appointment, I brought up the issue of lead. At my son's nine-month appointment, the pediatrician tested him again for lead, as is standard practice for this pediatrician's office. I fully expected the level to be at least a little elevated. I even hoped that it would be so that I would finally have the justification I needed to address the issue more seriously. But his blood lead level was still four.

Nevertheless, I continued to feel nervous.

At my son's one-year pediatric visit, I was still concerned enough about the lead that I requested an additional blood test. This time, his blood lead level was thirty-three, over three times the amount considered safe. A blood lead level of forty-five usually requires immediate hospitalization. Lead levels in the nineties can lead to seizures and even death. Later testing would reveal that the playroom was covered with an unbelievable amount of lead dust as a result of the stained glass work, and in between the floorboards were tiny pellets of lead. Some mysterious part of me *knew* that the house was toxic for my son. Yet I had been a "good girl." I let myself be silenced by financial worries and by my own internalized voice that told me I was irresponsible and childlike to put these fears first when we needed to be saving money. My dark imaginings about the lead were nothing more than irrational "womanly" fears, after all. There was no objective basis for my concern. A deep, timeless feminine knowing had alerted me to the danger to my son. But I had betrayed this part of myself by allowing it to be silenced. And it was my son who paid the price.

The full import of what this event meant for me and my soul was made clear to me by the following dream that I had some months after the diagnosis.

> *There is something wrong with my daughter—maybe she had a minor case of lead poisoning. My husband convinced me—rather, I let myself be convinced—that the best thing to do was to kill her. We put some poison in her bottle. She was lying there naked drinking it, and I was totally cavalier about it, kind of making jokes as I watched her pulse disappear. Then I suddenly realized what we had done, and I became enraged at my husband and was screaming at him for making me do this, but it was too late.*

The dream was shattering when I had it. It still sears these years later. In the dream, I have been compliant, and I let myself be talked into sacrificing some bit of tender feminine wisdom. It is significant that it is my daughter who gets sacrificed in the dream rather than my son, who, in reality, has borne the ill-effects of my self-betrayal. The instinctual feminine is imaged in the dream by my daughter. Becoming a mother awakened in me a new relationship with my feminine self. It was this feminine instinctual self that let me know the house was toxic, and it was she whom I betrayed. The dream husband is an inner figure—the internalized voice that causes us to doubt ourselves.

As I write this, my son is a teenager. There are no signs the lead harmed him, although I will probably never know for sure whether some light was extinguished during those months when his lead was elevated. I know that if I had not requested that third test, the exposure would have been longer and greater, and the outcome could have been truly catastrophic. Nevertheless, I know that I must not ever again shirk from claiming my feminine authority and wisdom, comprised as it is by both the intuitive understanding that defies rational explanation and the power and rage that allows us to stand our ground.

CLAIMING AGGRESSION

Claiming our authority will mean becoming comfortable accessing our capacity for aggression. We cannot stand in our knowing without a dose of healthy ferocity. Hence, it is absolutely dependent on our having confronted and integrated our shadow, as discussed in earlier chapters. When we can relate creatively to the dark, instinctual feminine, we can live a life that is full of vitality and authenticity.

Years after my son's diagnosis of lead poisoning, I had the following dream:

> *I am in a beautiful boutique, and in a lit glass case there is a priceless object carved in black stone. It is a gargoyle-type figure about the size of my fist. I somehow know that it was created as a ritual object and was used for religious purposes a long time ago. It hangs on a cord. I ask the proprietor if I can see it. When I put it around my neck, its eyes begin to glow red, and it comes to life. It attacks the people I am with, choking off their breath, so that they clutch at their throats. I am frightened, but I fight to control the figure. To do so, I speak to him in the same stern voice I use when trying to set a limit with my strong-willed*

son. It ceases its attack. My companions are all right. I have controlled this fiery power. I feel a little afraid, but also slightly exhilarated. The others in the shop agree that the totem obviously belongs to me by right.

Gargoyles originated with a medieval French legend of a fire-breathing dragon-like creature called the *gargouille* that inhabited the Seine, devouring boats and terrorizing villages. Saint Romanus subdued and conquered the creature with the help of a convict and brought its remains back to be burned. The head and neck would not burn, however, since they had been long tempered by the creature's own fire. This head and neck were thus hung on the cathedral to scare off evil spirits.

It is significant that the saint conquers the gargouille with the help of an outcast and criminal—the shadow. As we saw in part 2, the shadow contains hidden gifts. We need the fiery rage that is often disallowed, and we divorce ourselves from it at our peril. Just as in the legend, accessing disowned parts of ourselves can help us to conquer our demons in a way that produces something of lasting value. The terrifying gargouille becomes a helpful gargoyle. Its energy is no longer destructive but can be used for scaring off evil spirits and channeling water.

My dream is showing me how, as a mother, I had begun to learn to tap into my aggression and anger in a way that is in service to my authenticity. In part through my experiences of holding authority and even constructive aggression with my children, I was learning to access that side of myself in a way that made this tremendous power more available to the conscious part of my personality and could help me stand in my authority.

LOSING AND FINDING OUR HANDS

When we can listen to the deep wisdom of the archetypal old woman and claim some of her authority and understanding, we are better mothers. We are also closer to being whole. We live authentically. For many women, it may not have felt possible to claim our authority before having children. It was too painful or frightening to stand up to the voices that told us we didn't know what we were talking about.

And so we let our souls be gnawed at, and we didn't cause any trouble over these numerous tiny losses. But when we have children, our attitude changes. Suddenly there is another human being for whom we are responsible, and we know that we need to figure out how to start listening to ourselves or our children will suffer.

There is a version of "The Handless Maiden" in nearly all fairy tale traditions from Asia to Africa. It tells the story of a young woman who loses her ability to act in the world by having been sacrificed on behalf of her father, and how motherhood helps her to reclaim her agency. The following is the Grimm's version, although I have used the ending of the Italian version of the tale.

THE HANDLESS MAIDEN

A miller had fallen into poverty. One day, when he was out in the forest collecting wood, an old man stepped up to him and offered to make him wealthier than his wildest dreams if only he would promise to give him whatever was standing behind the mill. The miller told himself that only an apple tree stood behind the mill, so he agreed. The old man said that he would come in three years to collect what was promised.

When the miller got home, his wife greeted him excitedly and told him that every chest and box was filled with rich treasure. The man explained the bargain he had made with the old man, pleased with himself that he had gained such a fortune in exchange for an old apple tree. But his wife grew pale. "That must have been the devil," she told him. "He did not mean the apple tree but our daughter, who was sweeping the yard."

When the day came for the Evil One to come and take her away, the miller's daughter washed herself clean and drew a circle of chalk around herself. Therefore, the devil could not come near her. Angrily, he ordered the miller to take all water away from her so that she could not wash herself. Otherwise, he would have no power over her. Afraid, the miller did as he had been told. The next morning, the devil came again, but she had wept on her hands and they were quite clean. Again, the devil could not come near her. "Cut off her hands!" he demanded of the miller. Afraid for himself, the miller did as he had been told. The daughter, ever obedient, laid down both her hands and let them be cut off. The devil came for the third time, but she had wept so long and so much on the stumps that they were quite clean. The devil had to give up.

The miller's daughter announced that she could no longer stay with her father and mother, and she would seek a place in the world for herself. She walked and walked until night fell. Then she came to a royal garden filled with trees hanging with beautiful pears. Since she had not eaten all day, she reached up with her mouth and nibbled one hanging from a low branch.

The next day, the king to whom the garden belonged came and counted the pears and noticed that one was missing. That night, he concealed himself in the garden to detect the thief. When he saw the handless maiden eating a pear as it hung off a branch, he was overcome by her beauty. He approached her and asked her to accompany him back to his palace. Because she was so good and so beautiful, he loved her and made her a pair of silver hands. The handless maiden and the king were married.

After a year, the king had to go to war, so he asked his mother to care for his young queen. While he was gone, the handless maiden gave birth to two fine boys. The king's mother wrote a letter to her son, telling him of the happy news, but the messenger fell asleep and the devil exchanged the letter for another that told that the queen had given birth to a monster.

When the king read the letter, he was shocked and troubled, but he wrote back at once that his wife should be cared for tenderly. On the way to the palace, the messenger once again fell asleep. This time, the devil substituted a letter that instructed his mother to have the queen and his child put to death and preserve the queen's tongue and eyes as a token that she had obeyed. The old mother was shocked but could receive no further news from her son as the devil interfered with all attempts to reach him.

But the old mother wept to think that innocent blood should be shed. She had a hind killed and cut out her tongue and eyes and kept them. Then she sent the queen into the forest and instructed her never to return. The handless maiden had her children tied to her back and went away with tears in her eyes.

She wandered aimlessly through the forest for a long while until she came to a pool of water. Beside it sat an old woman. The handless maiden asked the old woman to draw her a drink from the pool.

"No," said the old woman. And she instructed the handless maiden to kneel down and drink.

"But can't you see that I have no hands? If I kneel to drink, my babies will slip off my back and fall into the water."

"That matters not," replied the old woman. "Go ahead and try."

The handless maiden knelt to drink, and as she did so, her babies slipped off her back and fell into the pool.

"My babies! Help me! They'll drown!" she cried, imploring the old woman for help. But the old woman didn't move.

"Have no fear," she said. "They won't drown. Reach in and pull them out."

"But how can I do that? I have no hands!"

"Then plunge your stumps into the water."

The handless maiden plunged her stumps into the water to rescue her children, and at that moment, she felt her hands growing back. She pulled her children out unharmed.

"Farewell," said the old woman. "Now you have hands and may do for yourself." And she turned and left before the handless maiden could even thank her.

The queen lived with her two children in a little cottage in the woods for seven years. One day, a man knocked on the door. He had a sorrowful aspect and was hungry and weary. He explained that he had lost his wife and two children many years ago and that he had been looking for them since. The queen revealed that she was indeed his wife, but he did not believe it at first since his wife had had silver hands. But the queen went into the next room and fetched the silver hands, which she still had in her possession. Then the king knew her, and the couple was happily reunited and lived in joy and contentment for all of their days.

Many of us have been wounded in a way similar to the handless maiden. We obediently comply with cultural or familial requests that we amputate some essential part of ourselves. We give up our hands—our ability to manipulate our world as we choose. Without hands, we have no agency and must be passive. The mutilation of the miller's daughter is a potent image of how women collude with the wounding perpetrated by the father. This can be a personal father with whom we have had a painful relationship, or it can be the negative aspect of the cultural father. In either case, the wounding agent is alive inside the psyche of the woman. We all carry our perpetrators inside us.

In fairy tales, the king usually represents the dominant collective values. When she marries the king, we see that the handless maiden can adapt provisionally to collective expectations. The silver hands also represent the "good enough" adaptation to the culture. They are something mechanical, not natural. They allow her to function better than before, and yet they are not truly authentic, not of her. The marriage to the king and the attainment of the silver hands represent an intermediate adaptation, not the happy ending.

When we have sacrificed our hands to the aspects of culture that require us to be compliant, it is too easy for our children to slip into the water, as my son did when I allowed him to become poisoned by the lead I somehow knew was in the house. But for many of us, we know that passively accepting our wounds is no longer an option when our children are at stake. The handless maiden has had an encounter with ancient feminine knowing—the goddess, for that is clearly who the old woman at the pool is. This deep, instinctual feminine wisdom will let her be passive no longer—not when it comes to the safety of her children. And when we strive with all our might to do something that before seemed impossible, but now we know we must attempt to save and protect our children, in that desperate moment we are healed. We have our own hands. We have grown into our authentic selves and live according to our inner authority.

HEALING

When motherhood calls us to be the best version of ourselves, we may, like the handless maiden, find that we have access to a miraculous healing potential that helps us reclaim our wounded agency. Catherine was a woman in my practice whose early experience of motherhood helped her find her way through extremely challenging circumstances. Catherine grew up poor in rural Georgia. Her mother was addicted to drugs and alcohol, and her father was mostly not in the picture. Catherine's early life was marked by chaos and dysfunction. Sexual abuse, violence, abandonment, and addiction were all part of her childhood experience.

When Catherine was fifteen, she became pregnant and decided to keep the baby. She has a vivid memory of being in her bedroom with her infant daughter. Her daughter was lying on the floor and Catherine was sitting beside her, looking at her. Even at her young age, Catherine had a keen sense of how her parents had failed her, and she felt a determination rise up in her that she would be a better mother to her child. With the birth of her child, her instincts for protection, survival, and flourishing asserted themselves. They expressed themselves in a particular conviction. Looking down at her daughter, she said out loud, "You will go to Harvard!"

This promise to her daughter became a kind of lodestone for Catherine. At some level, she grasped that she would not be able to lift her daughter out of poverty and chaos without getting herself out first. Though she had always been a talented student who had liked school and excelled, she was more determined than ever to do well and graduate. Though her father had rejected her in disgust after learning that she had become a teen mom, Catherine sought out his help to pay for college and didn't back down until he had agreed. While a supportive aunt helped care for her daughter, Catherine completed college. She eventually went on to get a doctorate in a highly competitive field and became an accomplished professional. In so doing, she took her daughter far away from the dysfunction of her family of origin, providing instead a home where there was warmth and stability. Catherine, in essence, kept her promise to her daughter, who was very accomplished academically and today works as a physician.

When her daughter was born, Catherine was a teen from disadvantaged circumstances who had already faced a great deal of trauma. She had few resources and little support. How could she manage to save herself, much less her daughter? Catherine's memorable declaration to her tiny child that day arose from an encounter with the inner guiding self. Just as the handless maiden's encounter with the old woman at the pool showed her how to claim her agency and authority so that she could heal herself and save her children, Catherine's encounter prompted her to take responsibility for her own life radically. "Now you have hands and may do for yourself," said the old woman at the pool. And somehow this realization was also gifted to Catherine when she recognized the enormity of her responsibility to her daughter.

Motherhood transformed Catherine. It transforms all of us in one way or another. It acts as a refiner's fire, burning away that which no longer serves. It demands of us that we show up for ourselves and our children. It is a call to become the person we were meant to be. Motherhood is an invitation to claim our wisdom and to stand in our knowing even against our self-doubt and the storms of criticisms from others. And when we can do this, we are released to pursue our authentic path, and our individuation story can unfold.

Questions for Reflection for Claiming Authority

1. Can you identify a way in which you have been taught to silence your instincts? How have you been able to access your instinctual wisdom while mothering? How has motherhood changed your relationship with your instincts?

2. In "The Hobyahs," the dog Turpie warns the family of impending danger, but the old man refuses to listen and instead punishes him. How have you ignored your own instincts about possible dangers in your life? How have you maimed your relationship to your instincts, perhaps by ridiculing or minimizing your doubts or fears? How has this affected your parenting?

3. At the end of "The Hobyahs," the hunter's dog eats up the evil Hobyahs. Where the little dog Turpie wasn't able to protect the family because he wasn't listened to, the hunter's dog is much more robust and effective. Sometimes when we have had the experience of being victimized in some way because we

didn't listen to our instincts, we quickly become much better at trusting them. Where in your life are your instincts robustly self-protective like the hunter's dog?

4. In "The Handless Maiden," the daughter willingly sacrifices her hands for her father. Many of us lop off parts of ourselves in order to meet the expectations of our families or our culture. How have you severed part of yourself? In what ways did this leave you maimed? How has this wound affected how you parent?

5. The handless maiden is unable to take care of herself at first. She must rely on the kindness of strangers. Many women go through a period in their lives where they look to others to provide care, direction, or guidance. How has this been true in your life?

6. It is only when her children are in danger that the handless maiden grows up—she gains her agency back when her hands regrow, and from that moment on, she is able to mother her children and care for herself. How has motherhood invited you to take more responsibility for yourself and your life?

7. The handless maiden is healed as a result of her encounter with the old woman at the pool. Where in your life have you been nurtured by contact with the wise feminine? Have you found such an energy in your inner world, your outer world, or both? How has a relationship with this energy been healing for you?

8. How has motherhood helped you reclaim your hands and find your inner authority?

Epilogue

The epiphany that seeded this book occurred over a decade and a half ago. I am no longer the same person who struggled with the double stroller on that bitter December day. Motherhood has changed me. I'm humbler, wiser, more confident, more tolerant, more open-minded, fiercer, and more courageous. I know much less about the world than I thought I did before I became a mother, but I also know more about myself. "If you seriously want to learn about life," notes psychiatrist and author M. Scott Peck, "having and raising children is probably the single best way."[1] Having and raising children is probably also the single best way to learn about yourself.

Motherhood is a doorway into your interior where you will meet the ghosts of old wounds, confront your darkness, and encounter your instinctual self. If you let it, it will take you down the deep well where you will have an initiatory encounter with the archetypal old woman. If you approach her with the right attitude—if you serve her well—she will shower upon you the riches of her wisdom.

What attitudes do you need to have to make the most of this encounter with yourself? In their book on parental attachment, Daniel A. Hughes and Jonathan Baylin suggest four key attitudes that can help us stay connected with our kids. Not by coincidence, these four attitudes also help us stay connected with ourselves, particularly when we are facing stress or challenge. These are summed up by the acronym PACE: playfulness, acceptance, curiosity, and empathy.[2]

Playfulness. To be playful means that we allow experimentation, flexibility, spontaneity, and joy. We make room for the unexpected. When you are experiencing difficulty—when you are sad, lonely, depleted, or angry—a playful attitude can be hard to cultivate. Do so, however, and you will be gifted a new orientation to whatever challenge you are facing. Playfulness shows up when you have reached the limit of your endurance and want to cry but find yourself laughing instead as you take in the absurdity of your situation. It appears when you think out of the box to overcome some impasse regarding yourself or your children. A playful attitude allows us to greet dreams, intuitions, and other communication from the unconscious with a warm welcome. We say, *What is this interesting image that came to me last night? What could it mean?* We play with the image and allow it to work on us. Playfulness is openhearted. It helps us to avoid getting stuck in an overly rigid, defensive position in which our conscious attitude must rule the day and be in control. When we are playful, we meet life with open arms, able to receive whatever gift is being offered. We are ready to embrace our adventure. Playfulness is the opposite of rigidity. You cannot be playful and rigid at the same time.

Acceptance. Finding acceptance for yourself when you are at your worst is no small feat. Motherhood will offer you many opportunities to do so. If you can cultivate an attitude of acceptance toward yourself even as you are struggling with some aspect of parenting, you will find yourself resting into a place of wisdom and transformation. "We cannot change anything until we accept it," wrote Jung. "Condemnation does not liberate. It oppresses. What you resist not only persists but will grow in size."[3] As mothers, we are challenged to accept ourselves for the mothers we *are*, not the mothers we wish we were. Our culture can have us believing that in order to be a good mom, we must excel at everything. We are supposed to be able to cook, organize, structure, mend, attune, set limits, play, clean, soothe, read, craft, nurse, attain, achieve, tutor, inspire, discipline, work, motivate, and any other number of things. In truth, we will have different strengths as mothers. You may have a gift for sharing ideas with your children but be an uninspired cook. You may be brilliant at getting your children to do chores but not be able to abide engaging in imaginary play. Accepting your particular genius along with your shortcomings is a radical act that will open up a more expansive sense of self. Acceptance is the opposite of disparagement. You can't be accepting and disparaging at the same time.

Curiosity. Deriving from the Latin word for "care," curiosity is perhaps the most important attitude to cultivate when engaging the inner life. Curiosity is the force that fends off the self-critical lashing. Instead of a torrent of self-abuse after making a mistake, you can turn toward yourself with curiosity: *I just yelled at my kid again. Let me get curious about that. What was I feeling right before I yelled? Has anything been on my mind today? I wonder what was happening for me?* When you do this again and again—when you make it a discipline to approach yourself with curiosity—you create space. Curiosity quiets self-blame, which in turn allows us to move into problem-solving mode. You can focus on why something happened and how you might be able to fix it or do it better next time because you're not so busy finding fault with yourself. In this way, curiosity brings us back to center and allows us to access our creativity in service to finding a new understanding or solution. The harsh inner critic must step aside as you move from self-censure to self-knowledge. You become an object of intense fascination for yourself and thus become aware that you are more complicated than you even thought. You learn to have respect for the complexity and paradox that exists within you. Even if we can't always like ourselves, we at least can find ourselves interesting and worthy of continued study. Curiosity is the opposite of judgment. You can't be curious and judgmental at the same time.

Empathy. Empathy for another allows us to feel into her pain. Empathy for ourselves means giving ourselves permission to experience our woundedness and suffering. Having empathy for yourself means that you treat yourself with tenderness and compassion. When you notice that your child is in distress, you probably tune in to her, express comfort, and invite her to tell you what is wrong. You can do this for yourself as well when you are in distress. Acknowledge that you are hurting, without any judgment as to whether you "deserve" to feel this way. Whatever they might be, give your feelings their full due. Welcome them and allow them to take up as much space as they would like while you are your own witness for these emotions. Feel them fully. Don't try to rationalize the feelings away under the guise of comfort. Don't tell yourself you shouldn't feel disappointed about your son's underachievement because you need to accept the child you have. Give yourself permission to feel the disappointment and offer yourself kindness and compassion while you do so. Once the feelings have had a chance to be fully felt, it will be easier to move into a place where you can challenge negative thoughts, see the issue in its proper perspective, and imagine creative solutions. Self-compassion helps us downregulate our nervous system and return to a state of relative equilibrium so that we can deal with whatever problem is on hand. In the Russian fairy tale "Vasilisa the Beautiful," the heroine's dying mother gives her a little magic doll. Whenever Vasilisa is overwhelmed, worried, or depleted, she feeds the doll and tells it her troubles. The doll then speaks, and says, "Go to sleep now, Vasilisa. For the morning is wiser than the evening." The doll is an image of an internalized good mother, who listens and provides the balm of empathy. You can be your own good mother, comforting yourself and reminding yourself that you will be able to meet the problem with fresh energy once you have taken good care of yourself. Empathy is the opposite of self-criticism. You can't be critical of yourself and show yourself empathy and compassion at the same time.

Playfulness, self-acceptance, curiosity, and self-compassion are the attitudes you will need on your journey down the well. For all the many years that you mother, these attitudes will always serve you well, but especially when the days are long and lonely. When we turn toward ourselves with curiosity, acceptance, compassion, and playfulness, we will have the tools to transform the dross of our suffering into the psychological gold of self-understanding. As you come to know yourself in all of your rich complexity, you will become wiser. Your openhearted stance toward life will enlarge and enliven you. Instead of finding bitterness and resentment, you will embrace life and come to love your fate. You will be well on the way to finding yourself and becoming the person you were meant to be.

Acknowledgments

The germ of an idea that was to become this book first occurred to me several months after the birth of my second child. Hence, this book has grown up alongside my children. Raising this book has had difficult, fretful moments, but there have been many along the way who supported me as I parented this creative project.

There were numerous Jungian colleagues whose assistance has been invaluable. Linda Leonard's writings have inspired and guided, and she was generous and encouraging at all stages. When I was stuck at the beginning, Susan Roberts listened patiently and then told me simply to start with a fairy tale. David Schoen, Frances Parks, and Phyllis LaPlante were early readers and shapers of this work when it was my thesis in analytic training. Puddi Kullberg has provided warm support and a heartfelt exchange of ideas. When I couldn't find the through line, Kaitryn Wertz was there—as always—to listen and reflect and aid me in finding my way. She helped me to articulate the central metaphor of the book and pointed me toward "The Two Caskets." I've always known I could turn to Joseph Lee for steady friendship, love, and hilarity. And Deb Stewart has been there from the very beginning, offering her gentle wisdom, generous perspective, and astute editorial guidance; I don't see how I could have parented either my children or my book without her friendship.

And there were others. When this project had been languishing and I was losing hope, the late Waverly Fitzgerald guided me in creating a viable book proposal. She later midwifed the birth of the introduction and first two chapters. She generously agreed to support me as I drafted later chapters. In her last months, as she was battling cancer, she read my daily installments and offered vital encouragement and feedback.

Stella O'Malley's friendship came at just the right time, and she has been both an inspiration and a support.

I owe a debt of gratitude to all of my clients—mothers and others. They've each taught me so much. I am especially appreciative of those who graciously allowed me to use their material in this book.

I'm so grateful for my agent, Adriana Stimola, who saw the value of this book right away and has lovingly championed it. I've appreciated her guidance and insight at every step.

I have been blessed to work with my editor, Haven Iverson, who made this book better in every way. I'm appreciative for her sensitive and astute contributions as well as her enthusiastic support. In addition, I'm thankful to the entire team at Sounds True.

And to Dom. Thank you for all of the blessings you've brought to my life.

Appendix

The fairy tales featured in this book come from across the globe. Many are very ancient. Below, I've listed them in the order in which they appear in the book and included a bit more information about the origins of the tales, along with some suggestions as to where you might go to learn more about each one.

THE TWO CASKETS

A Scandinavian tale that was originally collected by the British scholar Benjamin Thorpe. It appeared in Andrew Lang's *The Orange Fairy Book*. Similar tales include the French story "Diamonds and Toads." A particularly charming version of the tale from the American South called "The Talking Eggs" has been retold by Robert D. San Souci and wonderfully illustrated by Jerry Pinkney.

SELKIE BRIDE

A legend from Scotland. You can read more about it in *Mermaid and Other Water Spirit Tales from Around the World* by Heidi Anne Heiner.

THE SWAN MAIDEN

There are many stories about women who become swans. This one was collected by Joseph Jacobs. The folklorist D. L. Ashliman has a collection of this and other similar tales at his website at pitt.edu/~dash /swan.html.

DEMETER AND PERSEPHONE

There are different versions of the myth. I've referred to "The Homeric Hymn to Demeter," which was probably written in the seventh century BC. I first heard this story when my mother read it to me from

D'Aulaires' Book of Greek Myths by Ingri d'Aulaire and Edgar Parin d'Aulaire. This book has remained in print, and I was able to share it with my own children.

LITTLE BRIER ROSE

Sometimes better known as "Sleeping Beauty," this story comes from the Brothers Grimm. There is a version retold by Mahlon Craft and lavishly illustrated by Kinuko Craft, one of my favorite fairy-tale illustrators.

PRINCESS MOONBEAM

This version is related to the tenth-century Japanese story called "The Tale of the Bamboo Cutter." It is also known as "The Tale of Princess Kaguya." In 2013, the Japanese animators at Studio Ghibli released a beautiful full-length film of the tale directed by Isao Takahata.

THE SIX SWANS

This is another tale from Grimm's. A version of the tale published in 1998 features illustrations by Dorothée Duntze that capture the beauty and melancholy of the tale.

THE RAVEN

This is a tale from Grimm's.

THE STORY OF TWO WOMEN

This story comes from the Limba people of Sierra Leone and was recorded in 1961. It appears in Kathleen Ragan's anthology *Fearless Girls, Wise Women, & Beloved Sisters: Heroines in Folktales from Around the World.*

BIANCABELLA AND THE SNAKE

This is an Italian tale collected by Giovanni Straparola.

TATTERHOOD

This is a Norwegian tale collected in the mid-nineteenth century by Peter C. Asbjornsen and Jorgen Moe. I enjoyed sharing a 1993 version with my children retold and illustrated by Lauren A. Mills entitled *Tatterhood and the Hobgoblins*.

THE BLACK PRINCESS

This is a German tale that, as far as I know, has not been translated. Marie-Louise von Franz tells the tale and discusses it in her book *Animus and Anima in Fairy Tales*.

THE HORNED WOMEN

This tale comes from Ireland. It was collected by Lady Wilde and appeared first in *Ancient Legends, Mystic Charms, and Superstitions of Ireland*, published in 1887. It appears in Kathleen Ragan's anthology *Fearless Girls, Wise Women & Beloved Sisters*.

SWEET PORRIDGE

This is a Grimm's tale.

VASILISA THE BEAUTIFUL

This is a tale from Russia that was collected by Alexander Afanasyev. It has been famously illustrated by Ivan Bilibin. My favorite version is titled "Baba Yaga and Vasilisa the Brave." It is retold by Marianne Mayer and gorgeously illustrated by Kinuko Craft. Her rendering of Baba Yaga is deliciously creepy!

GLOOSCAP AND THE BABY

This is a legend of the Algonquin people. It appears in Jane Yolen's anthology *Favorite Folktales from Around the World*.

LORD KRISHNA EATS MUD

The story of little Krishna eating mud comes from the *Srimad Bhagavata Purana Book X*. Although it is difficult to date this text, it is likely from not later than the sixth century. The English translation I refer to is entitled *Krishna: The Beautiful Legend of God*, translated by Edwin F. Bryant.

RUMPELSTILTSKIN

Of course, this well-known tale is from Grimm's. My favorite version is retold and illustrated by Paul O. Zelinsky. The gold skeins shimmer in the illustrations!

THE STOLEN BAIRN AND THE SIDH

This is a Scottish tale. It is included in Kathleen Ragan's anthology *Fearless Girls, Wise Women & Beloved Sisters*.

THE HOBYAHS

This is included in *More English Fairy Tales*, by Joseph Jacobs.

THE HANDLESS MAIDEN

There are many different versions of this tale, and you can find some of these at Sur La Lune Fairy Tales, surlalunefairytales.com. I reference the Grimm's version for the first part of the tale, but I used the Italian version for the end of the tale. The Italian version is called "Olive" and is included in *Italian Folktale* selected and retold by Italo Calvino.

Notes

PREFACE

1. James Hillman, *The Soul's Code: In Search of Character and Callin* (New York: Random House, 1996).

2. Michael Meade, *The Water of Life: Initiation and the Tempering of the Soul* (Seattle: Greenfire Press, 2006), 20.

3. C. G. Jung, *The Collected Works of C.G. Jung*, vol. 12, *Psychology and Alchemy*, trans. R. F. C. Hull, 2nd ed. (Princeton, NJ: Princeton University Press, 1968), para. 6.

4. This is a paraphrase of a child's answer to the question "What is a myth?" as reported by Robert Johnson, *We: Understanding the Psychology of Romantic Love* (New York: HarperOne, 2009), 2.

5. Ami Ronnberg and Kathleen Martin, *The Book of Symbols* (Köln, Germany: Taschen, 2010), 610.

INTRODUCTION: JOURNEY TO THE SOURCE

1. C. G. Jung, *The Collected Works of C.G. Jung*, vol. 10, *Civilization in Transition*, trans. R. F. C. Hull, 2nd ed. (Princeton, NJ: Princeton University Press, 1970), para. 325.

CHAPTER 1 LOSING FREEDOM

1. Marie-Louise von Franz, *Puer Aeternus* (Boston: Sigo Press, 1981), 2.

2. Brooke Shields, *There Was a Little Girl: The Real Story of My Mother and Me* (New York: Dutton, 2014), 221.

3. Brooke Shields, *Down Came the Rain: My Journey through Postpartum Depression* (New York: Hyperion, 2005), 91.

4. Margery Williams, *The Velveteen Rabbit* (New York: Doubleday, 1991), 5–6.

5. Shields, *Down Came the Rain*, 156–57.

CHAPTER 2 LOSING CONTROL

1. Michelle Herman, *The Middle of Everything: Memoirs of Motherhood* (Lincoln: University of Nebraska Press, 2005), 153.

2. Herman, *Middle of Everything*, 205.

3. Herman, 199.

4. Herman, 200

5. Kahlil Gibran, *The Prophet* (New York: Knopf, 1923), 17–18.

6. *Black Swan*, directed by Darren Aronofsky (Century City, CA: Fox Searchlight Pictures, 2010).

7. *Black Swan*.

CHAPTER 3 LOSING OURSELVES

1. Daniel A. Hughes and Jonathan F. Baylin, *Brain-Based Parenting: The Neuroscience of Caregiving for Healthy Attachment* (New York: W. W. Norton, 2012), 13.

2. Katherine Stone, "Postpartum Depression and Postpartum Anxiety Help for Moms," *Postpartum Progress* (blog), accessed March 28, 2020, postpartumprogress.com.

CHAPTER 4 ENCOUNTERING DARKNESS

1. C. G. Jung and Aniela Jaffé, *Memories, Dreams, Reflections* (New York: Vintage Books, 1989), 247.

2. C. G. Jung, *The Collected Works of C.G. Jung*, vol. 16, *The Practice of Psychotherapy: Essays on the Psychology of the Transference and Other Subjects*, trans. R. F. C. Hull (Princeton, NJ: Princeton University Press, 1970), para. 470.

3. Nancy J. Dougherty and Jacqueline J. West, *The Matrix and Meaning of Character: An Archetypal and Developmental Approach* (London: Routledge, 2007), 57.

4. *Ordinary People*, directed by Robert Redford (Jefferson City, MO: Wildwood Enterprises, 1980).

5. C. G. Jung, *The Collected Works of C.G. Jung*, vol. 12, *Psychology and Alchemy*, trans. R. F. C. Hull, 2nd ed. (Princeton, NJ: Princeton University Press, 1968), paras. 421, 454.

6. Jung, *Collected Works*, para. 29.

7. Regina Abt, Vivienne MacKrell, and Irmgard Bosch, *Dream Child: Creation and New Life in Dreams of Pregnant Women* (Einseindeln, Switzerland: Daimon Verlag, 2000), 169.

CHAPTER 5 VALUING DARKNESS

1. Francois M. Mai, "Conception After Adoption: An Open Question," *Psychosomatic Medicine* 33, no. 6 (1971): 509, doi.org/10.1097/00006842-197111000-00004.

2. Marie-Louise von Franz, *Animus and Anima in Fairy Tales* (Toronto: Inner City Books, 2002), 67.

3. Regina Abt, Vivienne MacKrell, and Irmgard Bosch, *Dream Child: Creation and New Life in Dreams of Pregnant Women* (Einseindeln, Switzerland: Daimon Verlag, 2000), 79.

4. Daphne De Marneffe, *Maternal Desire: On Children, Love, and the Inner Life* (New York: Little Brown, 2004).

5. Kathryn Lynard Soper, *The Year My Son and I Were Born: A Story of Down Syndrome, Motherhood, and Self-Discovery* (Guilford, CT: Globe Pequot Press, 2009), 117–18.

6. Rozsika Parker, *Torn in Two: The Experience of Maternal Ambivalence* (London, UK: Little Brown Book Group, 1995), 69.

7. Parker, *Torn in Two*, 69–70.

8. Parker, 70–71.

9. Parker, 72.

10. Murray Stein, *Jung's Map of the Soul* (Chicago: Open Court, 1998), 107.

11. This comment was attributed to Jung by Jungian analyst C. Toni Frey-Wherlin.

CHAPTER 6 EMBODYING DARKNESS

1. Anna Quindlen, "Playing God on No Sleep," *Newsweek*, July 1, 2001.

2. Elissa Schappell, "Crossing the Line in the Sand: How Mad Can Mother Get?" in *The Bitch in the House: 26 Women Tell the Truth about Sex, Solitude, Work, Motherhood, and Marriage*, ed. Cathi Hanauer and Ellen Gilchrist (New York: Perennial, 2003), 202–3.

3. Susan Squire, "Maternal Bitch," in *The Bitch in the House: 26 Women Tell the Truth about Sex, Solitude, Work, Motherhood, and Marriage*, ed. Cathi Hanauer and Ellen Gilchrist (New York: Perennial, 2003), 205.

4. Squire, "Maternal Bitch," 205.

5. Squire, 213–14.

6. Elissa Schappell, "Crossing the Line in the Sand," 204.

7. Daniel Stern and Nadia Bruschweiler-Stern, *The Birth of a Mother: How the Motherhood Experience Changes You Forever* (New York: Basic Books, 1998).

8. Rozsika Parker, *Torn in Two: The Experience of Maternal Ambivalence* (London, UK: Little Brown Book Group, 1995), 137.

9. C. G. Jung, *Modern Man in Search of a Soul* (New York: Harcourt, Brace & World, 1980), 35.

CHAPTER 7 CLAIMING TRANSCENDENCE

1. Rainer Maria Rilke, *Selected Poems of Rainer Maria Rilke: A Translation from the German and Commentary*, trans. Robert Bly (New York: HarperCollins, 1981), 107.

2. C. G. Jung, *C. G. Jung: Letters*, vol. 2, *1951–1961*, ed. Gerhard Adler, trans. R. F. C. Hull (New York: Routledge, 1976), 525.

3. C. G. Jung, *The Collected Works of C.G. Jung*, vol. 14, *Mysterium Coniunctionis*, trans. Gerhard Adler and R. F. C. Hull (Princeton, NJ: Princeton University Press, 1970), para. 778.

4. C. G. Jung and Aniela Jaffé, *Memories, Dreams, Reflections* (New York: Vintage Books, 1989), 325.

5. Rachel Cusk, *A Life's Work: On Becoming a Mother* (New York: Picador, 2001), 42.

6. William Wordsworth, *Selected Poetry of William Wordsworth*, ed. Mark Van Doren (New York: Modern Library, 2002), 521–22.

7. Polly Berrien Berends, *Whole Child/Whole Parent* (New York: Harper & Row, 1987), xiii.

8. Dorothy Day, *The Long Loneliness: The Autobiography of the Legendary Catholic Social Activist Dorothy Day* (New York: HarperOne, 2017), 139.

9. Daphne De Marneffe, *Maternal Desire: On Children, Love, and the Inner Life* (New York: Little Brown, 2004), 313.

10. Cathi Hanauer, Ellen Gilchrist, and Kristin van Ogtrop, "Attila the Honey I'm Home," in *The Bitch in the House: 26 Women Tell the Truth about Sex, Solitude, Work, Motherhood, and Marriage* (New York: Perennial, 2003), 169.

11. Michael Gerson, "Saying Goodbye to My Child, the Youngster," Opinion, *Washington Post*, August 19, 2013, washingtonpost.com/opinions/michael-gerson-saying -goodbye-to-my-child-the-youngster/2013/08/19/6337802e -08dd-11e3-8974-f97ab3b3c677_story.html.

12. Gerson, "Saying Goodbye to My Child."

CHAPTER 8 CLAIMING CREATIVITY

1. Diane Mehta, "Sex and Sensibility," *The Paris Review*, October 16, 2013, theparisreview.org/blog/2013/10/16 /sex-and-sensibility.

2. Barbara Kingsolver, *High Tide in Tucson: Essays from Now or Never* (New York: HarperCollins, 1995), 96.

3. James Hollis, *Mythologems: Incarnations of the Invisible World* (Toronto: Inner City Books, 2004), 62.

4. Kingsolver, *High Tide in Tucson*, 95–96.

5. Theo Tsaousides, "The Thin Line Between Passion and Obsession, Part 1," *Psychology Today* (blog), October 25, 2016, psychologytoday.com/us/blog/smashing-the-brainblocks /201610/the-thin-line-between-passion-and-obsession-part-1.

6. Nina Winter, *Interview with the Muse: Remarkable Women Speak on Creativity and Power* (Berkeley, CA: Moon Books, 1978), 42.

7. Ian Parker, "Mugglemarch: J. K. Rowling Writes a Realist Novel for Adults," *The New Yorker*, September 24, 2012.

8. Parker, "Mugglemarch."

CHAPTER 9 CLAIMING AUTHORITY

1. Myla Kabat-Zinn and Jon Kabat-Zinn, *Everyday Blessings: The Inner Work of Mindful Parenting* (New York: Hyperion, 1997), 374–76.

2. Alice Eve Cohen, *What I Thought I Knew* (New York: Penguin Books, 2010), 44.

3. Regina Abt, Vivienne MacKrell, and Irmgard Bosch, *Dream Child: Creation and New Life in Dreams of Pregnant Women* (Einseindeln, Switzerland: Daimon Verlag, 2000), 50.

4. Jane Lazarre, *The Mother Knot* (Durham, NC: Duke University Press, 1976), 89.

EPILOGUE

1. M. Scott Peck, *In Search of Stones: A Pilgrimage of Faith, Reason & Discovery* (New York: Hyperion, 1995), 151.

2. Daniel A. Hughes and Jonathan F. Baylin, *Brain-Based Parenting: The Neuroscience of Caregiving for Healthy Attachment* (New York: W. W. Norton, 2012), 102.

3. C. G. Jung, *Modern Man in Search of a Soul* (New York: Harcourt, Brace, & World, 1933), 234.

Index

abandonment, 16, 66

acceptance, 81–82, 93–96, 204

Ackerman, Diane, 167

acorn theory, ix

adolescence, 61

adoption, 107–8

aggression, 193–94
  see also anger

alchemy, 91

alcoholism, 48, 73–74

anger, 117–22
  aggression, 193–94
  benefits, 126–30
  "The Horned Women," 122–24,
    134–35
  rage, 125–26, 134–35
  weeping, 130–33

the Annunciation, 148–49

archetypes, xvi, 7–9, 24, 81, 188–89

attachment, 59–60, 134, 203
  see also disconnection

"Attila the Honey I'm Home,"
    (van Ogtrop), 158–59

authority, 184

Baba Yaga, 133

Berends, Polly Berrien, 155

"Biancabella and the Snake," 91–93

Black Swan (film), 54–55

"The Black Princess," 109

blocked parental care, 60–61

The Book of Symbols, xvi

Brain-Based Parenting (Hughes
    and Baylin), 59–60

breastfeeding, 186–87

"Brier Rose," 42–47

Cassatt, Mary, 164

chronos and kairos, 157–61

Clifton, Lucille, 165

Cohen, Alice Eve, 187–88

commitment, 19, 31, 107

commitment, provisional, 23–24

control, loss of, 15, 35
  Black Swan (film), 54–55
  Demeter and Persephone, 39–41
  grief, 52
  Karen's story, 47–49, 53
  "Little Brier Rose," 42–47
  Monica's story, 35–38, 47
  "Princess Moonbeam," 49–51

cows (as symbols), 9

creativity, 163–66
  create, etymology of, 178–79
  demonic creativity, 170–72
  focus, 166–67, 175
  "Rumpelstiltskin," 168–70
  trusting yourself and your instincts,
    175–78

"Crossing the Line in the Sand:
    How Mad Can Mother Get?"
    (Schappel), 125–26

crying, 130–33

curiosity, 205

darkness, 3
  dark feminine instinct, 188–90
  as renewal source, 108–11
  see also anger; shadows

Day, Dorothy, 156
defeat, feeling defeated, 146–48
De Marneffe, Daphne, 110, 158
Demeter and Persephone, 39–41
demons, 170
depression, 71
    author's own experience with, x–xi
    Cassie's story, 94–96
    postpartum depression, 70–71
disconnection, 58–61
    Olive's story, 73–74
    Rachel's story, 58–59
    "The Six Swans," 61–68
doubling, 106–7
dreams, x, 2, 101–2, 109, 155, 179,
    185, 192–93
    dark feminine instinct, 188–90
    doubling, 106–7
    snake imagery, 92

empathy, 205–6

fairy tales and myths, xv–xvii, 2
    archetypes, xvi, 7–9, 24, 81, 188–89
    "Biancabella and the Snake," 91–93
    "The Black Princess," 109
    cows, 9
    Demeter and Persephone, 39–41
    doubling, 106–7
    "Glooscap and the Baby," 145
    gold, 5, 42, 64, 93, 102, 106, 143,
        168–69, 171, 177, 183
    "The Handless Maiden," 195–97
    "The Hobyahs," 184–85
    "The Horned Women," 122–24,
        134–35
    horns, 127
    "Krishna Eats Mud," 154
    "Little Brier Rose," 42–47
    mother-in-law as symbol, 68–70
    ordeals/trials, 81–82
    "Princess Moonbeam," 49–51
    Rapunzel, 109
    "The Raven," 84–85

"Rumpelstiltskin," 168–70
"The Selkie Bride" and selkies, 18–26
    sieves, 130
"The Six Swans," 61–68
    snakes, 91–93
"The Stolen Bairn and the Sidh,"
    176–77
"The Story of Two Women," 89–90, 93
"The Swan Maiden," 27–30
"Sweet Porridge," 128–29
"Tatterhood," 102–8, 111–15
    treasures/gifts, 135, 143, 183
"The Two Caskets," 3–7, 9, 81, 143,
    183
"Vasilisa the Beautiful," 133
    weaving/spinning, 4–5, 8, 43, 46,
        123, 126–27, 168, 171
    wells, xvi–xvii, 8, 15
    witches, 7, 61, 70, 104, 113–14,
        126, 129; "The Horned Women,"
        122–24, 134–35; "Vasilisa the
        Beautiful," 133
the Fates, 46
father wounds, 170–71, 174
focus, 166–67, 175
freedom, loss of
    Constance's story, 16–18
    "The Selkie Bride" and selkies, 18–26
    "The Swan Maiden," 27–30

gargoyles, 193–94
Gerson, Michael, 160
Gibran, Kahlil, 53
"Glooscap and the Baby," 145
God. See spirituality
gold, 5, 42, 64, 93, 102, 106, 143,
    168–69, 171, 177, 183
grief, 39–40, 52, 87, 134, 159

"The Handless Maiden," 195–97
Herman, Michelle, 41–42
hero's journey, xvi, 81
"The Hobyahs," 184–85

"The Horned Women," 122–24, 134–35
horns, 127

impatience, 84–85
Inanna, 3, 81
individuality, 29–30
individuation, xii–xiii, xv, 15, 136
the infinite. *See* spirituality
initiation, 1, 3, 8–9, 26
instincts, 175–78, 183–84, 188–90
   cultural impact on, 186–88, 197–98
   danger of not listening to, 187–88,
      190–93
   healing, 198–200
   "The Hobyahs," 184–85
isolation, 71–72

Jung, Carl, x, xii–xiii
   central fire, 161
   dreams, 2
   God/the infinite, 147–48
   persona, 86
   puella, 24
   shadows, 82, 99, 115
   the unconscious, 92

kairos and chronos, 157–61
Kali, 121–22, 126
Kingsolver, Barbara, 167
"Krishna Eats Mud," 154

Lazarre, Jane, 189–90
"Little Brier Rose," 42–47

"Maternal Bitch," (Squire), 129–30
Maternal Desire (De Marneffe), 158
Mehta, Diane, 164
The Middle of Everything (Herman),
   41–42
Mother Love, Mother Hate (Parker),
   112–13
motherhood
   abandonment, 16, 66

acceptance, 81–82, 93–96, 204
adoption, 107–8
anger, 117–22; aggression, 193–94;
   benefits, 126–30; "The Horned
   Women," 122–24, 134–35;
   rage, 125–26, 134–35; weeping,
   130–33
attachment, 59–60, 134, 203
defeat, feeling defeated, 146–48
disconnection, 58–61; Olive's story,
   73–74; Rachel's story, 58–59;
   "The Six Swans," 61–68
impatience, 84–85
instincts, 175–78, 183–84, 188–90;
   cultural impact on, 186–88,
   197–98; danger of not listening
   to, 187–88, 190–93; healing,
   198–200
isolation, 71–72
mother-in-law as symbol, 68–70
negative mother figure, 68–71
overprotection: Demeter and
   Persephone, 39–40; Monica's story,
   35–38
PACE (playfulness, acceptance,
   curiosity, empathy), 203–6
projection, 83–87
sacrifice, 20–21, 26, 29, 66, 146,
   198
values, reorientation of, 144
see also control; creativity; fairytales
   and myths; shadows; spirituality
myths. *See* fairy tales and myths

naming a problem, 172
narcissism, parental, 172–73
"nostalgia for the present," 158

ordeals, 81–82
Ordinary People (film), 86–87
overprotection
   Demeter and Persephone, 39–40
   Monica's story, 35–38
   see also control

PACE (playfulness, acceptance, curiosity, empathy), 203–6
Parker, Rozika, 112, 136
Persephone and Demeter, 39–41
persona, 86
Plath, Sylvia, 72
playfulness, 203–4
"Princess Moonbeam," 49–51
projection, 83–87
psyche, 5–6, 20–21, 23, 71, 92, 124
Psyche, 81
puella, 24

Quindlen, Anna, 121

Rapunzel, 109
"The Raven," 84–85
religion. *See* spirituality
renewal, 108–11
    see also darkness; shadows
Rowling, J.K., 174–75
"Rumpelstiltskin," 168–70

sacrifice, 20–21, 26, 29, 66, 146, 198
Schappel, Elissa, 125–26
Schumann, Clara, 164
the self, 15–16, 21–23, 29–31
"The Selkie Bride" and selkies, 18–26
shadows, 82–83
    accepting, 81–82, 93–96; Cassie's
        story, 94–96
    children, 111–14
    Ordinary People (film), 86–87
    positive shadows, 99–100; Selene's
        story, 100–2
    projection, 83–87, 112, 115
    "The Raven," 84–85
    reclaiming and integrating, 88–91
    "The Story of Two Women," 89–90,
        93
    "Tatterhood," 102–8, 111–15
    see also darkness; anger

Shields, Brooke, 22–23, 25, 30–31
sieves, 130
"The Six Swans," 61–68
the Skin Horse, 29–30
snakes, 91–93
Soper, Kathryn Lynard, 110–11
spinning/weaving, 4–5, 8, 43, 46,
    126–27
    "The Horned Women," 122–24,
        134–35
    "Rumpelstiltskin," 168–71
spirituality, 143–44, 147–50
    the Annunciation, 148–49
    Day, Dorothy, 156
    kairos and chronos, 157–61
    "Krishna Eats Mud," 154
    Laura's story, 151–53
    minnows and the whale analogy, 153
    ordinary versus the infinite, 153–55
    purpose and meaning, 156
Squire, Susan, 129–30
Stein, Murray, 114
"The Stolen Bairn and the Sidh,"
    176–77
Stone, Katherine, 70–71
"The Story of Two Women," 89–90, 93
"The Swan Maiden," 27–30
"Sweet Porridge," 128–29

"Tatterhood," 102–8, 111–15
time, 157–61
trials, 81–82
trusting yourself, 175–78
    see also instincts
Turpie the dog, 184–85
"The Two Caskets," 3–7, 9, 81, 143, 183

the unconscious, x, xvi–xvii, 7, 70,
    91–92
uniqueness, 29–31

values, reorientation of, 144

van Ogtrop, Kristin, 158–59
"Vasilisa the Beautiful," 133
The Velveteen Rabbit, 29–30

weaving/spinning, 4–5, 8, 43, 46,
    126–27
  "The Horned Women," 122–24,
    134–35
  "Rumpelstiltskin," 168–71
weeping, 130–33
Weldon, Fay, 117, 173–74
wells, xvi–xvii, 8, 15
Wilmer, Harry, xiii–xiv
wisdom. *See* instincts
witches, 7, 61, 70, 104, 113–14, 126,
    129
  "The Horned Women," 122–24,
    134–35
  "Vasilisa the Beautiful," 133
Wordsworth, William, 150

Yates, Andrea, 121

About the Author

Lisa Marchiano, LCSW, is a Jungian analyst, author, and podcaster. Her writings have appeared in numerous publications. She is the cohost and creator of the popular depth psychology podcast *This Jungian Life*. She is on the faculty of the C.G. Jung Institute of Philadelphia, and lectures and teaches widely.

Lisa lives with her family in Philadelphia. This is her first book.

About Sounds True

Sounds True is a multimedia publisher whose mission is to inspire and support personal transformation and spiritual awakening. Founded in 1985 and located in Boulder, Colorado, we work with many of the leading spiritual teachers, thinkers, healers, and visionary artists of our time. We strive with every title to preserve the essential "living wisdom" of the author or artist. It is our goal to create products that not only provide information to a reader or listener but also embody the quality of a wisdom transmission.

For those seeking genuine transformation, Sounds True is your trusted partner. At SoundsTrue.com you will find a wealth of free resources to support your journey, including exclusive weekly audio interviews, free downloads, interactive learning tools, and other special savings on all our titles.

To learn more, please visit SoundsTrue.com/freegifts or call us toll-free at 800.333.9185.

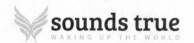